I Got Your Message!

Understanding Signs from Deceased Loved Ones

Joseph M. Higgins

Part of the Always Connected Series

I Got Your Message!
Understanding Signs From Deceased Loved Ones

Copyright © 2014 Joseph M. Higgins

Always Connected LLC

All Rights Reserved
No part of this book may be reproduced or transmitted in any form or by any means without written permission from the author.

ISBN-13: 978-0-9825716-2-0
ISBN-10: 0-9825716-2-3

Printed in U.S.A.

This book is available at quantity discounts for bulk purchases.
For information, contact www.josephmhiggins.com

Acknowledgements

I would like to acknowledge all the people who supplied stories for this book. By sharing your story, you will help bring peace and healing to many who read your personal loving connections.

I would also like to thank their deceased loved ones who, by sending them a sign, let all the readers share in this loving contact.

As always, I need to thank my teachers and guides for helping me with the presentation, information and insight which is found in this book. Without your continuous support, this book would not have been possible.

Dedication

This book is dedicated to those whose hearts are broken by the physical loss of a loved one.

May this book bring some peace and healing to your struggle to understand the separation of the physical does not mean the end of your connection to your loved ones.

You are *Always Connected*

Table of Contents

Introduction
    Channeling Explained
    Always Connected

Section I	1
What Are Signs?	3
You Are Not Alone	9
Bereavement & the Afterlife	15
Section II	21
How And Why Things Work	21
The Process	23
How It Will Be Done	25
Where It Will Be Done	27
When Will It Be Done	29
Why Do They Come To Us?	31
Why Not A Sign?	33
Can I Ask For A Sign?	35
Increase My Chances Of Getting A Sign	37
What's On Your Mind?	41
What Is Learned From Signs?	41
Signs Are Not Religious Unless...	44
Can A Sign Be Sent If...?	47
Do Children See Signs More Than Adults?	50
How Do We Know If It's Authentic?	52

Section III	55
Particular Methods To Gain Your Attention	55
Use of Birds, Butterflies and Lady Bugs	57
A Bird & Butterfly	61
Moms Favorite	63
The Owl	64
Cardinal	65
Morning Dove	66
Use of Coins	69
Hello	72
Mom's Coins	73
Canadian Penny	74
Pennies From Heaven	76
Use of Numbers	79
Friday the 13th	83
The Clock Alarm	84
The Hawks	85
Skeptic No More	86
Use of Feathers	91
Moms Feather	96
Pet Sign	97
The Bus	98
The Interview	99
Use of Special Occasions	105
The Dress & Play Time	110
The Bell	112
The Anniversary Gift	113
Use of Voices, Inflections & Thoughts	117
Inflection	121
Mom's Voice	122
Asked in a Letter	123

Asked for Help	126
The Greeting Party	127
Use Of Shared Signs – Group	129
A Friend's Aunt	135
Winter Cardinal	138
Tree of Life	139
Five Way Calling	141
The White Flowers	142
Use of Personal Items	145
The Rug	150
The Buffalo	152
The Beatles	153
Eternity	155
Multiple Methods	157
Section IV	161
Other Examples of Signs	161
Dreams	165
Mom's Message	165
Watching Over Me	165
Smells	169
Grandad is Here	169
Electricity	171
The Door Bell	171
Phil's Cell	172
Wake Up!	173
Just Saying "Hi"	173
Music	175
Mustang Sally	175
Multiple Signs	177
Other signs	181
The Mammogram	181

Loving Energy	182
Grandpa & Jake	183
I'm going Too!	184
The Picture Frame	185
Email from Heaven	186
Always Connected	189
Section V	193
Webpages	193
Other Books by Joseph M. Higgins	193
Hello ... Anyone Home?	194
The Everything Guide to Evidence of the Afterlife	195
Always Connected For Veterans	196

Introduction

It has always been my desire to be able to share my knowledge and experiences with those in need, in hopes of bringing peace and healing. This new book is part of this process. I wanted to connect with a large portion of the population who can relate to the possibility of After Death Communications, (ADC). It is also focused on those who are looking for answers to some of the experiences that they have witnessed themselves. By having people share their stories about receiving signs from their deceased loved ones, they too are able to prove that our loved ones are still part of our lives and can reach out and contact us.

The information that I have received from my guides and teachers is always welcomed, and the knowledge that they transfer through me to the readers is always important and desirable. We always have questions and concerns about life and the possibility of an afterlife. By giving access to the general population the knowledge that has been transferred to me, and by including individuals' personal stories of contact with the deceased loved ones, I am able to add to the knowledge that we currently have about the afterlife.

I wanted to add this book to the Always Connected Series because it is a great example of how our loved ones, even though physically gone, are still connected to all of us here. It is a great example of how death cannot separate the loving connection we share with our family and friends.

I hope you enjoy the information contained in this book, as

well as the stories that have been so generously supplied in order to help bring peace and healing into your lives.

Channeling Explained

The concept of channeling is best explained by my guides in my first book, Hello…Anyone Home?

As for the technological explanation of how a channel works, that is something that we can explain to a certain extent; but, at times, it may seem to be discombobulated.

We have analyzed the thought waves and mechanisms that Joseph's biological structure uses on a daily basis. Further, we try to interact with these thought patterns in order to mix our thoughts in with them so that he might understand the information that is coming from our side.

Once there was a general recognition of how Joseph's particular pattern works, we were able to intercede and stimulate certain mechanisms that alerted him of our presence. Over time and with much patience and practice Joseph has learned to accept our invitation to communicate. He has trained himself to put his conscious focus to one side so that we may input data into his conscious mind for him to transcribe and to understand.

We see that this method of communicating is much more efficient than other methods such as communication through dreams, as the information that we need for him to transfer is of such an amount that single, individual contacts would prohibit this process."

Always Connected

Channeled from Joes guides

We want to convey to everyone the knowledge that each and every one of you is always connected. You are all connected on a spiritual level. And yes, you are all connected on a physical level. On a physical level, you all share the same physical plane. At this time, you all live on a living structure you call Earth; in the future, you will share living on other structures. Your physical bodies basically consist of all the same elements, so there are many common connections between you and every other physical being with whom you interact.

On a spiritual level, which is much broader than the physical level, you share similar attributes. You share a similar spiritual existence. The makeup of your spiritual being is similar to that of others with whom you interact, and your ability to learn and create experiences is similar to that of others.

So not only are you connected on the physical and spiritual levels, but you must realize that at no time are you alone. We realize that there are times in people's lives when they feel as if they're totally alone, both physically and spiritually. This is never the case. You are always interacting with others, either physically or spiritually and either consciously or subconsciously. Your spiritual entities are in constant contact with others on our plane who help guide you through your existence and journey on the Earth plane. There is never a time when you are alone on your journey and do not have access to help from others on our plane. You are always connected, you always have been connected, and you always will be connected.

Section I

Be prepared to realize who you really are ... A loving spiritual entity, not the body you currently occupy.

J.M.H

What Are Signs?

When you accept a sign from our side, you are actually affirming your own true existence as a beautiful spirit who learns that there is no death.

J.M.H

Channeled from Joe's guides

Signs are a method we use to communicate from our side, or what you might call the afterlife, and your side. At times, we have attempted to communicate through other methods, some of which were successful, while others were a total disappointment. An example of one of the other methods of communicating with you was through the use of astrology, or the alignment of certain heavenly bodies surrounding your planet. Some of these techniques are used today, but not as they originally have been intended.

That particular method was misunderstood as it was interpreted by individuals who were not the individuals to whom the signs were directed. Often what happens is when a sign needs to be interpreted by a third-party, it can become skewed and distorted. Throughout history well-meaning individuals and those who had less than the best intentions manipulated the signs due to ignorance or self-advancement.

So we learned quite some time ago to try to use very personal signs associated with the deceased loved one that only the individual who was to receive them would understand. We branched this method out so that signs could also incorporate family and friends, and even groups when that particular method was necessary.

So it was decided that individual signs would be the best method to communicate from our side to yours. As generations went by, some of these signs became well-known to the point where we are still able to use them today, as they have been recognized already as a method of communication.

An example of this, which we will explain later in this book, could be the use of coins, feathers and the animal kingdom. By past generations accepting the signs as coming from the afterlife, it has made it easier for current generations to recognize the signs and therefore be more willing to accept them.

Because recognizing a sign is the first step in the communication process. If one recognizes that a sign is possibly from a deceased loved one, it opens the lines of communication to the point where acceptance, that is belief, can be achieved.

If we try to use a new method of communication, it would have to be something that was extremely specific to both the individual who has passed and the one remaining on the Earth plane. Therefore, these other forms of communication are limited in their use. This may take the form of direct communication through voice. Some individuals are able to be used as a conduit between our world and yours. They are able to bring messages through, using the actual voice of the deceased loved one. These messages can be shared with an individual or group. These individuals are rare and used mostly for demonstration purposes to show that this method still exists and can be used when necessary.

So the use of signs as a communication method has resulted in the understanding that, once one passes from the Earth plane existence back to their spiritual body, they can still communicate with those who have been left behind.

In this book we will talk about many common signs we use to transfer this communication. Some of you may recognize some of these and have actually experienced the use of these methods. For some others, these methods may be new or misunderstood. We hope to bring understanding surrounding these methods to all, in order to take the mystery away from how and why we use this method.

Signs are also a very easy form of communication. They are usually very short, precise and specific. This makes them easier to understand and accept. At times, a sign can be more complex and involve other methods of communication. But these methods are not the norm and are used in specific situations. Everyday signs that occur to millions of people have been practiced, sharpened and then perfected over time.

With each generation we build on the communication that we have used in the past. We continually work on new methods of communication and some of you alive today will see these before it is your time to pass over. These new methods will be used through the science of communication. By this we mean communication methods that you use among yourselves on the Earth plane. We have been working on these for some time, and your technology only now has begun to enter the phase where we can implement these methods at a high level of success. The meaning of this method of communication will be evident when use becomes open to the general population.

So for the purpose of this book, we want to focus on the simple method of sending and receiving signs between the living and those living on the spiritual plane. Many of these methods will be recognized by those reading this book. It is our intention to just give background and understanding to these methods without going into the scientific makeup of the transfer of the message.

Some of the stories you read in this book have been picked out by us in order for you to understand, in a practical way, how that particular method plays out. Also, it is important for those reading who have experienced signs themselves to see how others have also experienced similar signs.

The signs we use are of a universal nature. By this we mean we can use some of these signs in all cultures and geographic locations on your plane of existence.

Some are specifically altered to the particular region or beliefs of that culture. But the methods are the same, meaning we try to use objects and memories of each individual involved in the transfer of the communication.

Perhaps in one culture, a particular object or event might be used to send a sign that would not be used in a different culture. The method is the same, but the particular object or symbol would be different.

So it is important to remember that not only are people in your particular culture or country receiving signs from the deceased loved ones, but all humans throughout the Earth plane can and do receive signs from the afterlife. And we use the word afterlife to signify a deceased loved one sending a sign back to the living loved one. Signs are still communicated from our side, which is the spiritual dimension of life, to your plane of existence by guides and teachers in order to help individuals and groups grow and learn.

You Are Not Alone

According to Pew Forum/survey on Religion & Public Life recent polls, over 20 million people have felt as if they had received a sign from someone on the other side.

How many people in the past have received a sign? We'll never know. But with today's technology, polling techniques, the willingness to be more open about this type of subject, they can get a pretty good understanding of how many people have had some type of interaction. Now, that number is just in America and does not include other countries.

It also doesn't include people who believe that this can happen, but it has never happened to them personally. For those of you who have not received a sign, hopefully you will, if you want to.

And I add that" if you want to" because some people accept the process and the belief that it's possible, but don't want to be contacted for various reasons. We'll go over some of those reasons when we talk about the process, and on how everything works later in the book.

What this shows is you're not alone in your experiences with receiving signs from your deceased loved ones.

Channeled From Joe's Guides

Joe, the reason why we contact so many people in order to

send them a sign is basically that each individual has questions about the afterlife and the existence of their deceased loved ones.

Each individual has their own thoughts, beliefs and experiences with the death of the human body. Some will have specific beliefs concerning this aspect of the transition, while others will immediately think of the person that was attached to that particular body. By this we mean the actual personality of the person or persons who they love.

So we try to reach out to as many as possible with this method of communication in order to answer some of those questions concerning the belief in the continuity of life. We use other means to also answer some of these questions. But for this book, we would like to focus on the signs we send to individuals and groups to let them know that life continues after the change called death.

What is important to understand is that the individual is not alone in experiencing these types of phenomena. We try to keep certain methods and concepts in sync with certain beliefs and cultures. This makes the methods of contact more universal and agreeable to those who will witness them. Many times people think they are alone in experiencing this form of communication. Some will even try to not accept the fact that these signs of being sent, for they believe others will think they are mentally unbalanced.

In years past, many individuals were grouped together and

placed in confinement for their belief that they were in communication with the afterlife. Various degrees of isolation and persecution were inflicted on these individuals throughout time. This has caused us to be more selective and secretive in the communication process so those receiving the sign could find comfort that their loved one still existed and continued to be able to communicate with them from the other side.

They could hold onto this knowledge individually without sharing it and still gain the peace and healing that was intended when the sign was originally designed to be sent.

As people became more aware of this method of communication and begin to share their experiences among close friends and family members, the power of the signs grew. Family members felt more secure talking about it amongst themselves without others outside their circle of trust being privy to the information.

This began the long transition of sending and receiving signs to individuals that would hold this particular communication method to themselves. As the ages moved along and the sharing of this information became much more publicly acceptable, the methods and frequency of this form of communication increased.

This is one of the reasons why we have Joe writing this book. To continue to advance the awareness that these signs are currently being sent from our side to yours. With the age of technology, more people are able to share their experiences concerning these particular methods.

As more people share their experiences, more people will come forward and share theirs, thus expanding the awareness of the process.

There are many places still on the Earth plane where this type of communication is frowned upon, and where it even can cause disturbances that could be harmful to the individuals who mentioned their participation.

But it is our intention to spread this information as far and wide as possible during this time on the Earth plane. We want to let as many people know as possible that they are never alone in their experiences.

These experiences are part of your spiritual makeup. As one would send a postcard or letter or, in this day and age, an e-mail to a loved one or friend across a continent or world, we can also do this from the afterlife to the plane of existence you're currently on. The method is the only thing that is different.

Someone might not have seen someone for 20 years and then contact is made doing e-mail, or perhaps through a common friend and soon a connection is made. If one passes to our side, they too can send a message, in this case a sign, to a loved one that they have not seen in a while.

So the concept of communication is just a matter of tweaking different methods to see which ones work best with each individual. But overall, these methods will be used throughout the population on the Earth plane.

An example of this is that we are like postal workers in that we deliver messages. Some messages are delivered and accepted, while others are lost and some are even "stamped return to sender" if they do not wish to be accepted for various reasons.

One should believe that life continues after the change called death and that it is just a matter of tuning in to the best method in order to receive communications from that plane of existence. We have found that simple signs from your deceased loved ones to yourself are the easiest form of communication. So we will continue to use this method throughout your plane of existence as we test, adapt and implement other means of communications to be used now and in the future.

Bereavement & the Afterlife

Channeled from Joe's Guides

Joe, we would like to give you some information concerning bereavement and its association with the afterlife. When someone loses a loved one by their transitioning back to this spiritual state of existence, the ones who are left behind begin what is called the grief process. This process has many stages and can begin before the actual transition of the soul.

Many times, if a family member or friend is close to passing over their loved ones will realize that time is short and that they will lose this loved one very soon. Therefore, they begin the grief process even before the loved one has transitioned back to our side. Some individuals have a higher threshold of separation and will wait until after the passing of the individual.

It all depends on the individual's makeup and their experiences throughout their life on how they handle the situation when a deceased loved one crosses back over to their natural state. Many times, other close family members and friends will help and assist with the grieving process as the situation occurs.

Many times this grief process works in combination with one's religious beliefs, cultural beliefs or even how they believe or think about the afterlife. Many individuals have different insights and beliefs in these areas, and therefore the outcome of the grief assistance, as well as the grief process itself, will vary between different cultures.

Joe what we wish to discuss is the association between the loss of a loved one and the continuation of life back to our plane of existence. You see life does continue from your dimension onto ours. The exact scientific makeup is much more complex, but for this type of explanation concerning one's loss of a loved one, we will try to put it into context of this book.

When people enter the bereavement stage, what they are actually grieving over is the loss of the physical body which housed the spiritual soul of the individual. People living on the Earth plane live with the association of matter and substance. People associate living beings with a physical presence.

As some people miss their loved ones while they are away on a trip, or perhaps have moved to live in a different location when they lose a loved one permanently back to our side, the permanent nature of such a transition can cause much distress for those left behind.

The physical body that houses the soul is a structure made up of chemicals and materials that are found on your plane of existence. As with all things on your plane of existence, these materials can be fragile, broken or decompose.

This is the makeup of your world. However this body

structure is only used as the housing for the spiritual entity that you call your loved one.

You see the actual person that you love is not the physical housing of the body, but the spiritual entity that lays within. That is why it is so important to continue to grow and experience life on your plane to add to your own personal spiritual essence.

Many people put too much emphasis on the physical body and equate success, or perhaps superiority over others due to their physical attributes. This is an illusion made up by man in order to serve other individuals who put the value of the body above the value of the spiritual entity.

But when one passes over, the physical body can no longer be judged or equated with one's status in life as it had been throughout their lifetime. So the real essence of the individual, their spirit, is what is remembered. People remember loving memories, thoughts, and interactions of the particular person more so than the physical being. From the time of birth, one's physical body will continue to change, but this spiritual makeup will remain stable throughout their lifetime. Through their experiences and actions, this spirit can grow more compassionate and see life with a higher level of wisdom.

So it is important for people to realize that just because one's physical body ceases to exist does not mean that this spiritual essence has also ceased to exist. People have a tendency to think if you cannot see it or touch it, it does not exist.

Of course, this is very simplified, but many people experience this with the passing of a loved one.

Humans are very connected in the sense that they interact on a physical level very often throughout their existence. This can start at birth with the mother and child being in close proximity, all the way through the procreation of new children, and throughout the lives of the individual in their social, cultural and learning experiences. So the individual from the beginning of the birth is constantly in physical contact with others throughout their life. So when one pass over to our side and that physical contact is no longer able to be implemented, those around the lost loved one begin to feel as if their life is incomplete without the ability to see or feel the physical being of the one who has passed.

But when one passes back to the spiritual side of life, they still have access to the physical plane of Earth. They can still interact with those that they have interacted with throughout their lifetimes. The communication methods and interactions are different than when in the physical plane. Although physical manifestations and physical contact can be implemented, most times the communication is limited.

By understanding this concept, one can realize that once the physical body is no longer of use, the spiritual entity who crosses back to the spiritual side of life will continue to live their life to the fullest. They have the ability to remember events during their life on the physical plane as well as all their loved ones, friends and coworkers. The way they see things once they have left the physical body is much more in perspective to what really has happened during their experience on the Earth plane.

By this we mean from their new perspective on the spirit side of life they can see how certain events worked out, how certain relationships were developed and how love was felt between individuals. This gives them an extra edge in seeing how their lives are really played out when they existed on the physical plane.

So when people reach the bereavement and grief stages on the physical plane, it is important to realize that your loved one is still in existence, but now in the spiritual state on a different plane of existence. The plane of existence for which they are now located is still within the grasp of their loved ones who remain on the physical plane.

This means they can be in contact with them, they can feel their sorrows and joys, and can be with them for all their milestones and celebrations. And they will be watching over them and interacting with them at certain times throughout the remaining years of their life. The grieving over the loss of the physical body is understandable due to the interaction between individuals living on the Earth plane. But what one must remember is that the person who you interacted with still exists, still loves you and still is part of your life. This information needs to be used and accepted in order to decrease the grief that one experiences with the loss of a loved one. Use this knowledge, knowing that your loved one is as close and dear to you as when they were on the physical plane.

In all actuality, they are even closer to you than when they were actually living on the physical plane. Because they can be with you at any time or all the time, depending on your thoughts, emotions and wants.

Section II

How And Why Things Work

You are not limited in communicating with our side…
you just think you are.

J.M.H

The Process

The first step is what I call the Evaluation Period.

This is the time frame when, after a loved one passes, certain decisions are made. Some of the decisions that have to be made are:

- Will a sign be given, if at all?
- When will it be done?
- How it will be done?
- Where it will be done?

When a loved one crosses over, they go through a stage of acclimating to the new environment. There are guides and teachers that will help them with the communication process if a sign is determined to be sent.

So they will evaluate the situation at hand. They will decide if it is the right time, and who might be best to receive a sign.

Once the decision has been made (by the individual, teachers and guides), if the sign will be sent then they must decide how it will be done.

How It Will Be Done

This process will begin with evaluating the deceased loved one's entire life and coordinating certain memories that are associated with themselves and to the person who will received a sign.

One of my favorite ways of explaining this is: It's like walking down the aisle in the supermarket. And all the products on all the shelves are different parts of your life. One might be a birthday, honeymoon, favorite food, a humorous event, or a particular item. So they will take a particular memory that is associated with your loved one and use that as a possible sign to send to you.

An example of this might be someone who loved fishing; they had all the special equipment, they read all the books, and they shared their joy of fishing with those around them. When a sign from them comes through, there is a good chance it might be associated with something to do with fishing.

But if this particular person had no interest in, say, horse racing, they're not going to send you a sign about a horse race. Unless of course you're at the races and one of the horses name is "dad's gone fishing." Then that's probably a sign for you.

So they are going to use something that is familiar to you about them.

Channeled from Joe's Guides

Joe, we have the ability to see and feel the memories of the living loved one. With this ability, we are able to pick the proper associated items or events that have the best chance of being received. These events and items may slightly differ from individual to individual. An example of this is a wife may remember a specific trip or event that brought laughter to the family. A son or daughter of the same family may remember the event or trip in a slightly different manner, or perhaps a different aspect of it. So if we used the same trip or event to send a sign to both the wife and a child it would be sent according to how that individual remembered it. The slight variations in the sending of the sign are needed in order for the sign to have a better chance of being recognized and accepted.

Where It Will Be Done

Memories of certain places are very important to us. It may be a trip or honeymoon, a place you both shared together, or perhaps his or her favorite place. Some of us love the beach, others love the desert. Some people love the serenity of the woods or even one's back yard. So if you're in that environment and the thought of a loved one comes to you, there is a greater chance they were using the actual place as a stepping stone to get your attention.

Channeled from Joe's Guides

Joe, we try to use locations that will help in the acceptance of the sign. By this, we mean locations that are associated between the living loved one and the individual that has passed, but also locations where other connections such as emotions could heighten the ability of the sign to be accepted.

The environmental conditions are also very important in the location where we choose to attempt the passing of the sign. If a particular location, even if it has all the criteria of a shared memory, is too loud or distracting to the living loved one, a sign will not be attempted, as it may go unrecognized or perhaps even cause confusion to the receiver. This confusion can corrupt the process later on when a different sign may be attempted to be sent.

It is important that we have the opportunity to use all the tools that are available to us. Outside sources of distraction can easily manipulate some of these tools and decrease the power. While living on the Earth plane, the human body is very sensitive to outside stimulus -- such as loud noises colors in the interactions with other individuals. These are some of the things that we must overcome when sending a sign. So when a location is picked, all of these particulars must be taken into account in order for the sign to be received successfully.

If one is trying to increase their chances of gaining a sign from a deceased loved one, it is highly recommended that a peaceful, stable mindset be utilized. An example of this would be one that was experiencing a calmness, serenity associated with being in a peaceful mood. Also being an environment where distractions are limited. A familiar saying on the Earth plane is "I can't hear myself think." You don't want to be in an environment where you "can't hear yourself think," as this will make the attempt at sending a sign and receiving it very difficult.

When Will It Be Done

Sometimes signs are sent right after passing. This could be due to your total focus around the individual. Your attention is not taken away by outside stimulus like your weekly TV shows, things at work, the daily drama that usually surrounds our lives. So it's easier for them to get a sign through right away.

Channeled from Joe's Guides

Joe, when it will be done will also depend on the individual's belief in the possibility of receiving a sign. Those individuals who are more open to the possibility and to understanding the concept of receiving a sign from a deceased loved one will have a better chance of connecting with the deceased loved one soon after the passing. Some individuals, even though they are in the midst of the grieving process, are open enough to not only receive, but to accept the sign. While others would not be able to even receive a particular sign, due to their emotional environment.

However it's a double-edged sword; it also can be the hardest time to get a sign. People are emotionally upset, they're anxious; they can be tired and stressed. A sign can be met with confusion and cause additional anxiety and misunderstanding. So they will hold off and try at a later time.

Sometimes they come through other family members or even friends. Because they know the family members or friends will pass this information on to you at the proper time. This is not uncommon, as it has happened in my own life and possibly in yours.

Why Do They Come To Us?

- To say they're okay
- "They made it"
- They still exist, still love us and will be with us throughout our life
- To show support at an appropriate time in relation to the current situations that are happening in our lives.

Many times, we ask if a loved one is okay, where they are, if they still remember us. So these are the reasons they like to send a sign just to let us know that they're still around.

To say they're okay: When a loved one passes over, we all want to know if they're okay, or if they are in pain and suffering. Because many times when we are at the stage of leaving the Earth plane to return to a natural spiritual state, the human body may not be performing at its peak level. So the fact that a sign can be received brings great warmth to us, as we know our loved one feels our uncertainty and tries to relieve it.

"They made it:" Often times we are not sure where a loved one has gone. All we know is that the physical body has ceased to function and we are no longer able to communicate with them. By receiving a sign we can be assured that they have made it to the next location. Something as simple as a small sign can bring us great relief knowing that they have made it to the other side, even though we do not know exactly how that process works.

They still exist: The ability for a loved one to send us a sign proves that they still exist. They no longer may be a part of the human body, but their consciousness continues and they are able to communicate to us. So, on some level, even though we may not be able to comprehend what kind of existence, we know that they are still real.

To show support: Many times they will send a sign at an appropriate time when we need their support in dealing with a particular situation. This allows them to show us that they are still with us, love us, and will be around to support us throughout our lives. It is very comforting to know that we can tap into our deceased loved ones for strength during stressful periods in our lives. Comfort that they brought to us on the living Earth plane can still be accepted after they have crossed over. They want to show us that their love for us, their concern for us, still exist.

Why Not A Sign?

- The person might not be ready, emotionally or mentally for contact.
- Their culture or religion may hold them back from accepting a sign.
- Their doubt is so strong that there would not be capable of accepting a sign.

An initial sign, or even signs at any time, may not be given due to various reasons such as:

Religious beliefs: I've had people tell me that they believe in signs, but that their religion does not allow it. So they are reluctant to ask and accept a sign.

People are too distraught: They may be in the middle of the grieving process and any attempt at sending a sign may cause more harm and confusion. If it is believed that a sign would bring discomfort, it would be delayed or even not allowed to happen at all.

Subconscious doubt: Even though an individual says they may be comfortable, and receiving a sign from a deceased loved one subconsciously, they could have major doubts about the process or even if it should be done at all. They may be scared of receiving a sign, as they think you may be associated with unpleasant entities from the other side. Or even that may be disturbing the deceased loved one. Their mind will create these barriers, even though their conscious mind says they are willing to accept such a possibility.

At times, individuals who have passed will be so anxious to send a sign that they will not obey the guidelines and attempt to send the sign on their own. Frequently this ends up scaring or confusing the recipient.

Can I Ask For A Sign?

Yes, by asking for a sign you are giving them an invitation to make contact.

You can do this through a simple prayer, or just thinking of them will open up communications.

Be open to the possibility. Believe. Be willing to accept the sign that you receive. Remember to say thank you; it lets them know you have truly accepted the sign and will increase your chances of getting more signs.

Some people are just naturals at receiving and understanding signs. They just overwhelmingly believe that they happen and are truly thankful.

We all have a tendency to question ourselves if this was actually a sign from a deceased loved one. So we asked for another one, and then another one and then maybe one more. Listen, I've done this myself, and I should know better. So once you receive and recognize this contact, take it as a sacred event between you and your loved one. And think about the bigger picture of our lives. That life continues and love transcends death.

When you ask, ask with NO expectations. Don't put conditions on it, like how you want the sign, when you want it or where.

No conditions

I once had a lady who wanted to ask for a sign, but she told me that they shouldn't send it the following week because she was going to be on vacation. And to try not to send it in the afternoon because she might be at her daughter's soccer practice. Like they didn't know her schedule!

Now I bet they were rolling their eyes on the other side thinking that this woman just doesn't get it. So when you ask for the sign, let it go, and let them do the hard work. Don't put any conditions on it.

Increase My Chances Of Getting A Sign

One of the techniques to increase your ability to receive a sign is the ability to put yourself in a relaxed state of mind. Meditation is one of the best ways to open up the communication highway to make contact. But for the average Joe, I like to tell them to be aware of the times when a sign may come through.

Some of these times are at night when you're sleeping. Dreams are the number one way for our loved ones to contact us. We are more relaxed, they have access to memory processing configurations, and they can use visuals much more easily.

I also found that daydreaming is a perfect way for them to access you while you're awake. Other forms of meditation that can be done besides the ones you sit in silence are:

- Gardening
- Listening to music
- Reading
- Painting

Or anything else that relaxes you to outside stimulus. In sports, they call it being in the zone, meaning you're very focused and you have the ability to shut down outside stimulus. So the everyday person can also set up the atmosphere of being able to be contacted by not only meditation, but also participating in a hobby or action that they can feel like they can get lost in.

With these types of activities, you will increase the chances of communication at a higher level, perhaps even hearing sentences which could develop into conversations.

Channeled from Joe's Guides

Joe, we have talked about putting yourself in the right frame of mind in order to increase the probability of receiving a sign. But we think it's also important to mention that one does not necessarily have to believe in the process before it happens to actually work. By this we mean, if someone is willing to be open-minded enough to accept the sign that has been given to them, then this in itself will create other opportunities for future signs to be given.

Sometimes people wish to continually receive signs from our side. Unfortunately, this does not increase the communication between both sides. Once one expects signs from a particular loved one, it puts a damper on the original meaning of the sign that has already been received and accepted. By asking for additional signs under normal circumstances, it decreases the value of the first sign that was accepted.

What more could you want to know than your deceased loved one still exists and still is able to contact you?

If you need to be constantly contacted through a sign, it truly means that you have doubts that the signs you have received were true. Otherwise, by accepting the reality of the original sign, you have proven that your belief is without doubt.

If, however, you're going through a particular difficult time during your life on the Earth plane, additional signs can and will be sent in order to support your belief that your loved ones and guides are looking over you and supporting you during this difficult time. You see, in this case, a sign is used to bring love and support. So it has a specific purpose in its intention.

But when people want additional signs just for the sake of having a sign, the intention is now not necessary and a sign may not be sent.

If you continue to be thankful for the signs we send and appreciate the timing of a particular sign, then your loved one may wish to continue this method of communication. They can hear and feel your loving thoughts and concerns, and they will decide when additional signs will be sent.

If you have never received a sign and wish to receive one, following some of the information in this chapter such as simply asking for a sign and being open to believing in the process, will help in the configuration and presentation of the sign.

If your energy keeps an open line of communication with your deceased loved ones, this in itself will increase the ease with which a sign can be transferred to you. Sometimes a sign is meant to be sent but the person's physical energy being low or confused will not allow a sign to come through. But if you can keep your energy at a higher level, meaning a more simple and pure level of love and compassion, then the sign can come through with more ease.

Your emotional energy plays a large part in the transferring of signs. Release your worries and doubts that are around you during your daily lives, and put yourself into a peaceful state of non-judgment of yourself and others and this will facilitate the receiving of the sign.

Some people may wish to design their own sign. We often hear people ask for a sign to be given in one particular manner. We take this request seriously and will try to adapt the configuration of the sign to meet with their guidelines. However, if there are other circumstances that the individual is not privy to that may interact negatively with the sign, then that particular method will not be used. Keep your mind clear of your intentions and ask for a sign and we will do our best to facilitate the communication between you and your deceased loved ones.

What's On Your Mind?

When a person passes over, your love for them doesn't end, why would their love for you end?

J.M.H

What Is Learned From Signs?

Channeled from Joes Guides

Joe, the question you have chosen is a wonderful question that reaches deep into our reason to transfer this information. Learning who one is is an ongoing experience for spirits on your plane of existence. By transferring information through signs, we can bridge the gap between our world and yours.

Most people go about their daily lives without thinking of who they really are as spiritual beings. But when the signs are received from a loved one who has recently passed, it brings home the understanding that we are all connected on a certain level.

People may not understand the signs, but they begin to ask questions as to the meaning of the signs. This opens up a window for us to teach you that you are part of the bigger picture. Some may not want to accept the fact that a sign is being given from our side, while others are more open to the possibilities and are willing to accept this communication for what it is.

By us sending and you receiving this communication through the act of a sign, we have opened the dialogue for you to realize that your life existence is ongoing, even when you consider the death of the physical body.

A sign can teach you the many possibilities that are available in living your life. By this, we mean the understanding that things are not always as they seem. Actions, events and situations play out on many different levels, and many times people don't understand this.

By understanding the transfer of signs from one plane to another, we have given you the opportunity for you to understand your place in existence. You are not alone in a physical body going through your life making indiscriminate choices, and then ceasing to exist.

Your existence continues after the physical body decomposes, and you continue on in your learning experiences at a higher level. By sending signs, we have made you aware of the fact that life does continue, and that we can reach back and communicate with your plane of existence to let you know that this is in fact the truth.

Some people, when realizing that these communications clarify who they actually are and how life continues after the physical death of the body, will change the way they are leading their life. Their course of action may be abrupt, and other times they may cause the individual to ponder and think of how they wish to spend their limited amount of time on the physical Earth plane.

This is a great opportunity to be able to understand one's life purpose, knowing that your existence will continue. The short time you experience life on the Earth plane will become more precious.

Some will accept this fact and use this to their advantage in moving forward in bringing peace into their life. Others may be skeptical and discard what they have seen and experienced, and this is a lost opportunity to bring the reality of your existence to the forefront.

If you realize that your existence continues and the life lessons you have learned will be brought forward into your new existence, how would you live your life? Would it be to bring compassion and help to others, or would it be to take advantage and create suffering. These are profound questions that need to be answered by each individual.

Every individual has personal experiences that need to be anchored in their knowledge of afterlife. By doing this, it gives the soul the opportunity to grow at a faster pace and achieve higher levels of understanding. By not taking advantage of this knowledge and understanding the possibilities, one is limiting themselves to just the experiences they have been involved in on the Earth plane.

By sending signs, we are actually giving you a beacon of light in order for you to realize you are not alone, and that we can still interact with you and help you on many different levels. But most often, it is just the act of realizing that a deceased loved one has not really ceased to exist, but has traveled on to their new plane of existence. This plane of existence has the ability to communicate and interact with the physical Earth plane. Your love transcends the death of the physical body. We can feel your emotions, both good and bad.

We hear your prayers, we hear your sorrows and we enjoy your accomplishments. We share with you celebrations and milestones that continue in your life on the Earth plane. Just because we cannot be seen or be there in the physical body does not mean we are not here at all.

But we do want you to live your lives, as it is your individual responsibility to learn and grow and accept the challenges that the Earth plane has put in front of you. We just wish to remind you that, by accepting the signs we send to you, we are giving you access to the larger picture of your own existence.

Signs Are Not Religious Unless You Want Them To Be

Channeled by Joe's guides

Joe, when we talk about the concept of signs we want to

make it clear to everyone that we are not choosing a particular group of people who will receive the signs over another group who will be left out.

Unfortunately, many of your religions isolate their members from others in the general population. This can be seen in the current activities surrounding you at this time. Sometimes these groups will even go to extreme methods in controlling the sources of information that are allowed to be received by their members.

We do not accept or condone these practices, but we will interfere with these practices if it becomes necessary in order to facilitate the growth of a particular group. There are various reasons why these groups would not allow signs to be understood by their members. Some would lose the power of controlling their members to a higher authority which they could not control.

In order for us to reach as many people as possible through the use of signs, we will use different groups and religions in order to facilitate the acceptance of the sign. By this, we mean we can integrate a sign that is acceptable to the group as a whole.

We do not, however, have to use a particular religion's ideas in order to send the signs.

It's just easier for some people to accept the meaning of the signs we send if it is integrated with their particular religion or group. The main goal is to be able to send a sign and for the individual to accept it.

If this means that a particular sign must be integrated into that particular person's religion, then we will attempt this.

This doesn't mean that signs that we send are associated with a particular religion. It just means we are using that situation in order for the individual to be able to accept the sign.

One does not have to belong to a particular religion or group in order to receive a sign. But we will often use a person's membership in a particular group to help with the acceptance of a sign.

If one particular person is very religious or very aligned with a particular group, then we may use a method that is related to this particular religion or group. If this is the only way that the individual will accept a sign, then we may use this technique.

However, no affiliation to any group or religion is needed for one to receive a sign from a deceased loved one. One may be an individual not associated with anyone else and still be able to indulge in the wonderful aspects of receiving a sign.

The methods of transmission of signs are many. So we look for common factors when determining how and when a sign is to be sent. So we want to make it clear that, if someone needs to have a sign associated with a particular religion, we will try to make this happen. But otherwise, when a sign is sent we will try to make it more particular to the individual who is sending it, as well as the one who is receiving it, without any affiliation to another group.

If signs are being sent to a whole group at one time, then of course the association with that particular group will be a main theme in how signs are sent in its makeup. But individual signs to individual people are not religious-based, unless the person either receiving the sign or the deceased loved one who is participating in sending a sign would be associated very strongly with that particular religion.

We did not judge others religions or groups when trying to facilitate a sign. The most important aspect of a sign is the ability of it to be recognized and accepted. We will use any method that will cause this action to be achieved.

Can A Sign Be Sent If One Were Unable To Communicate On Our Side?

Channeled by Joe's Guides

Joe, the physical limitations that you perceive on your side are not observed on our side. What you consider roadblocks, or the inability to communicate with one another due to physical limitations, is not a concern once you reach our side. By this, we mean someone that is not able to speak or to communicate to others on your plane are able to communicate very well once they have crossed over.

Some people who have limitations on the physical plane are able to perceive things at a higher level, meaning their understanding of situations can be more acute than the average person. They have access to other senses that others do not tap into, for they have the ability to communicate more easily using the physical senses.

Once someone that had a problem communicating on your side crosses over, we are able to teach them the mechanisms needed to send a sign to their loved ones. The signs may include actions that you may perceive to be of the communication concept.

By this, we mean signs may include abilities that the deceased did not have while living on your plane. An example of this is someone may hear their name being called and associate it with the deceased due to the timing, environment, or the expectation of receiving a sign. This may seem inappropriate, as the deceased may not have been able to speak; however, it would be appropriate for them to come through with a sign that is audible, to show that their limitations are no longer valid.

Many times people who have disabilities that affect their ability to communicate with others on your plane become exceptionally gifted communicators when they reach our side. This is because they are more acutely aware of their surroundings when on the Earth plane, and wish to express their feelings to others. On our side, they have this ability and therefore use it. What they lacked on the Earth plane is used as a teaching method to others who may have had trouble communicating on the Earth plane.

These people also have the ability to teach those still living on the Earth plane how to deal with their lack of communication skills. They may intervene in certain circumstances in order to help the individual communicate certain needs, wants, and desires. They perform these duties through various methods, such as thought manipulation, awareness stimulus, and oftentimes through the dream state.

There are mechanisms in place for communications to be present in the here and hereafter for those who need it, study it, and manipulated it. When we use the expression manipulated, we mean to integrate it into other abilities and senses. This happens so that meanings and understandings of certain events and feelings can be shared with others.

It's important to understand that communications mean many different things to different people both on your side and ours.

On your side, it is the main way of sharing ideas, problem-solving, and social interaction. On our side, communication is the ability to be aware of one's surroundings and to realize one is connected to many different sources, and that this information and connection can be shared beyond the physical and spiritual boundaries.

Do Children See Signs More Than Adults?

Channeled by Joes Guides

Joe, the ability to connect to our side is available to all those who believe it is possible. Some individuals have a difficult time understanding the concept of communicating between your side and ours. Others are more open to the possibility, and therefore have the ability to accept the process and possible outcomes.

When children first enter into the Earth plane, they bring with them many tools and experiences that they have learned on our side. They may not be able to utilize these tools in their current state of development, but they are still part of their essential makeup. They have the ability to feel and sense at a higher level than most adults.

As a child, they have the ability to be inquisitive without the fear of being judged. They can interact with our side much easier, because they have less expectations and have not been burdened by society's strict norms.

They learn from this ability at the beginning of their life on the Earth plane. As they grow older, some of these abilities to sense and understand one's surroundings are often lost to more visual stimulus, as well as the interaction with adults.

It is possible for children to connect with us on multiple levels while still learning to communicate on your plane. They do this through the senses of intuition and thought. They have a primary way of connecting back to where they had come from, and this form of communication usually does not develop further as they begin to age.

However, some adults do continue to learn and use this source of communication throughout their lives. This ability may lay dormant for others and appear later on in one's life to be studied, or even perhaps set to the side.

People should also realized that the soul is in a conscious state before birth, after birth, and in-between incarnations on any plane. So the soul is aware of other entities that they may be around, including others who have been within their existence at other periods of time. An example of this might be the term used as a soul group. This term has been simplified for many to understand -- the concept of souls interacting with each other.

In actuality, the individual soul is always in connection with all the other souls, but at different levels of contact. Your essence is continuously mixing with the essence of other souls during many time frames and dimensions.

How Do We Know If It's Authentic?

A real sign will cause a real emotional response, a WOW moment. The kind that gives you goose bumps.

A vivid dream that lasts many years, one that you can still remember the details like it was last night.

You're thinking of your deceased loved one and then all of a sudden bang, there's a sign

Once they come through, they might repeat contact at the same time, place, and use the same sign. Examples of this are finding coins, repeated smells associated with your loved one, or perhaps sequential numbers showing up at a particular time every night or early morning.

Oftentimes, we doubt ourselves if we have actually received a sign. Even though we might be open to the possibility and truly believe that we can receive a sign, often this will reduce the quality of that sign when you accept it. The strong loving connection is weakened by your doubt.

Many times, the signs will be blatantly obvious to us and others around us. We might think that they would not send such an obvious sign, when in reality the signs can be huge, or as small as a whisper. So if you truly believe that contact has been made, you can be reassured that it is authentic sign. For if you truly believe, a loving connection is developed between our side and their side, even if the sign that you have recognized was not originally authentic. Just by truly believing a loving connection can be made, it will cause a sign to be actually instigated and created by ourselves.

If a sign is received around a particular special event such as a wedding or the birth of a child, then there is a higher probability that the sign is authentic. Our deceased loved ones love to show that they still are in our lives, and therefore will attempt to send signs around times of family gatherings or moments of remembrance. Holidays, birthdays, and specific places all can add to the weight of judging if a sign is authentic.

Section III

Particular Methods To Gain Your Attention

If you could send a sign to a loved one, who missed you with all their heart, and thought you would not be in their life anymore, wouldn't you try?

J.M.H

Use of Birds, Butterflies and Lady Bugs

Channeled by Joe's guides

Joe, at times we like to use the animal kingdom and nature as a method in communicating a sign from our side to your side. We have used this method many times throughout history. It is easy to access an individual's attention and understanding when using this method, so we continue to use it when it is appropriate.

When we say appropriate, there are times when other methods are more convenient and more understandable than the use of animals or parts of nature. But in this case, we will discuss the use of certain birds, butterflies and ladybugs.

The concept of birds being used as a source of communication has been handed down throughout times. In modern times, cardinals and certain other species have been known to have a connection from the Earth plane to the afterlife. Other birds in other cultures are used to communicate a sign, depending on what in history has been used before. By this we mean certain species are associated with the afterlife in particular cultures, and these are the ones we use when trying to send a sign to an individual who belongs to a different culture.

Cardinals have been very much used as a communication

method as people understand their significance in transferring a sign. Their appearance can be quite striking, especially when used against the backdrop of snow and ice. This is also one of the reasons for use of this particular bird, because their appearance gains the attention of the individual immediately and focuses their mind on that particular object. The association with the deceased loved one is then planted in the mind of the living loved one so as to make a connection.

When the living loved one begins to associate a deceased loved one with a particular bird such as a cardinal, then any further signs are accepted more readily and without hesitation. The person only has to have an awareness of the history of a particular bird such as a cardinal in order to begin to accept the possibility that this bird is creating a sign from a deceased loved one.

Once that connection is made we can use this particular method throughout one's life during different occasions in order to make contact. The bird may appear before a certain event, or perhaps during a stressful time in one's life -- or even around a special occasion such as a birthday. The connection will be immediately understood and, therefore, the sign will be readily accepted.

Often times we use insects such as ladybugs, as they also had a history of connection to the spiritual realm. Many believe that the ladybugs have special powers or are associated with certain events or emotions. These understandings can shift between cultures but are all used to our advantage in trying to communicate to your side. Ladybugs are often used because they are very distinct in their colors and size. When one sees ladybugs, they know exactly what it is at first sight. The individual does not have to think or analyze if this particular insect is what it is, or perhaps something else. So the thought process does not have to proceed in an analytical way, which could interrupt our ability to send a sign to the loved one. It is one less obstacle for us to overcome in trying to communicate with your side.

Often, children at a young age are introduced to certain species in order for them to understand the natural world. Ladybugs are often used as an example of a particular insect or being part of the natural landscape of one's environment. Children will easily accept this particular species, as the colors and size of the particular insect is non-threatening. Children are often drawn to this particular insect because of their colors and how they stand out against the surroundings.

Often, children are allowed to let the ladybugs actually crawl on their hands. This is a first-hand experience for the child in learning new things about nature. The ladybugs become even more non-threatening, and in turn become emotionally attached to the young child.

So we are able to use this particular object later on in life to send a sign from our side to yours. As these children grow and become adults and bring others onto their life plane they, too, teach their children about nature and ladybugs in particular.

Butterflies have always been a sign of change and development throughout time. They are also associated with signs from deceased loved ones on our side. The butterfly in its essence is created from what seems like two different life forms. The caterpillar, which then becomes the butterfly. The caterpillar, like the ladybug, is often used to teach young children about the natural world.

Children are allowed to play with caterpillars to a certain extent, and by this their interaction with them is close and meaningful. As the child's knowledge of the caterpillar increases, they realize that the caterpillar will change into a butterfly at some point in its life. Having witnessed, touched and experienced the life of the caterpillar they are more inclined to follow its growth into a butterfly.

When the butterfly is created, it also has a range of colors and distinct markings that can gain the attention of anyone whose presence it comes into. One does not need to be directly involved in the study of nature to understand, or to accept, a butterfly for what it is.

The actions of a butterfly as well as a ladybug are non-threatening, as many children have learned early in life. Adults also will continue with that experience and enjoy the presence of each of these. Many times we will use the butterfly as a simple sign that your loved one is around you. It is a non-threatening, non-stressful and easily understood sign that is used quite often around the world and throughout history.

As the understanding of the use of these three particular participants of nature, as well as others, such as the dragon fly, continues to grow, it makes it easier for more people to understand the symbolism of their makeup in order to pass a sign on from our side to yours. As people teach their children about these particular insects and birds, the process continues from generation to generation.

So when you come into contact with a particular bird or insect, such as a ladybug or butterfly, just remember they stand for more than a part of the natural world. In actuality, they are used for not only teaching others about the history and connection to the afterlife, but are also used directly to send a sign from our side to yours.

When we send signs from deceased loved ones, or perhaps even a guide or teacher to an individual on your side, we want the sign to be recognized as well as be accepted. By using particular birds, ladybugs and butterflies, we have a greater chance that our presence will be recognized very quickly.

Through the history of association that has been passed down throughout time, the probability of the acceptance of a sign associated with the deceased loved one is very high, and thus we will continue to use this method.

A Bird & Butterfly

My Dad passed in 2004. A couple of the things he

enjoyed was to help around in the yard and he knew all the types of birds in the area.

Well, during that summer my husband, Paul, had a bird following him all around the yard ... even sitting on the back of his riding mower every time he had to mow the lawn. Anytime he did any project, the bird was there ...Paul would always talk to him when he did projects. And when Paul had a problem he would say: "Dad, could you please help me out" ...Paul would say: "I don't know why I do that, but it works"...Thanks dad for helping out!

The week after my mom passed in April, my neighbor took me to get a plant. She said she wanted me to have something that reminded me of mom.

So I picked a beautiful butterfly plant. I always said to mom laughing: "Dad came back as a bird, so I want you to come back as a beautiful butterfly."

The next day, Paul, my husband, was planting the bush, and said: "Come on Grammy" (he called her that since we had kids).

Before he was even finished planting, a beautiful butterfly landed and stayed on the plant the whole time he planted it...We were in shock. Thanks Mom!

DEB

IN MEMORY OF MOM AND DAD

Author's Comments

When people really believe in the continuation of life and readily accept signs from their deceased loved ones, then these signs will continue to be seen, heard and felt. In these two cases, there is still interaction between the living and the deceased, as when Paul asks for help in the yard, or asks for "Grammy" to come to the new tree.

The deceased loved ones have found the connection using what their kids would associate with them. The father knew all the types of birds in the yard, so Deb knew he was into birds and so the perfect sign.

They listen to us, and in these cases, they replied.

Moms Favorite

> *I went to the cemetery last summer with my brother to visit my parents' graves. The annual air show was over in Quonset that weekend. I was looking up in the sky and said Dad and Mom give me a sign. My brother thought I was crazy... and I will admit it today.*
>
> *Just then, two airplanes went over and dipped their wings. My brother looked at me with confusion on his face and I just smiled. I said: "Ok dad, now what about you mom?" And as we looked down on the grave marker, a ladybug (moms favorite) walked right across her name on the stone. Not anyone else's but hers! I*

thought my brother was gonna die. I just smiled ... Now he believes!

Deb

Author's Comments

It's great when a sign happens; it's even better when there is someone else there to witness it. In this case, a brother who was somewhat skeptical, to say the least. But her parents made it clear enough to convince him in the end.

And this was the purpose of these signs -- she was already a deep believer in signs from our departed loved ones. Being in that location, with his sister, and getting two signs from mom and dad provided a perfect scenario to give him a glimpse into the possibility of an afterlife.

It was personal, it was family and it was seen by someone else he trusted. It all worked together to open his eyes to the wonderful possibility of life after death.

The Owl

A medium told me my husband was going to send me an owl. I was skeptical, and she e-mailed a few days later to ask if I'd seen the owl yet. I hadn't. But the next morning I woke up to an enormous white owl in a tree outside my window. We live on a farm and I had never seen an owl here before — and in the daytime! I got dressed and took my dog outside and the owl was still there. As we walked by, he flew off. He was enormous. Great snowy owls are very rarely spotted around here.

JOAN KATHERINE CRAMER

AUTHOR'S COMMENTS

Mediums can bring through valuable information from a deceased loved one. Sometimes in the messages they pass on information about an upcoming sign, such as in this story, an owl. This was a way for Joan to know for sure that this unusual sign was truly from her deceased loved one.

Cardinal

I read online that if you see a cardinal it means your loved ones are near. I looked outside that day and said: "I wish I could see one as a sign you're (my parents) still with us. I had not seen one all winter.

Then I walked outside to take the garbage out and I looked up and there it was, a beautiful cardinal sitting on the fence. I said thank you!

Then, as I am typing this story for Joe, another cardinal is sitting on the deck looking in the window right now! Wow!

DEB

Author's Comments

Cardinals are used often to signify that a deceased loved one is around, or trying to say "Hi." The fact that many people realize this helps them in this method of communication. In the past, they had used other birds, depending on the culture and location of the deceased. If a loved one is familiar with a particular bird or animal, they will use that as a sign, since you already know of the connection between them and their familiar subject.

Morning Dove

When I need my dad or just want to see if he's around, he always comes through on various occasions.

We had a huge family reunion at our house one year and I wished that he would be here with us, because we had a hundred of his relatives in our yard having a wonderful time. He always loved having people around him.

I relate my dad to a morning dove that was on a wire when we moved into our house 14 years ago. When we first drove into our driveway, the bird was on the wire. And every day from there on out, he was there. My husband was cooking and that lovely bird was walking on the top of the deck border as he was cooking two feet away.

Bob had to come find me to show me, and it brought so much comfort knowing Dad was here with all of us for the party!

Laurie

Author's Comments

When our loved ones pass over, one of the biggest regrets we tend to have is that they are not with us for family gatherings. That is farthest from the truth. They love to attend get-togethers and feel the loving energy that is produced in these circumstances. The fact that they often show us signs is a great relief to all of us that witness such events. Often, many will share in these signs, while at other times, it's like a private message from them to us in a crowded room.

Use of Coins

Channeled from Joe's Guides

The reason why we like to use coins as one of the methods for sending signs from our side is that people recognize the value of the object and are less likely to miss it once they're aware of it.

The fact that the coin is worth something in your material world helps us in gaining your attention and focus on this particular object. Some may say the coin appearance is just a coincidence. However, this is not the case. We have taken particular actions to acquire this coin, and relocated it into the path of the desired loved one.

We do not wish to associate the monetary value of that particular coin with the value of the loved one. The denomination is irrelevant to the sign. We are trying to gain your attention by usingan object that is considered important in your society and gives us an edge in gaining your attention.

Other methods are used for other purposes in other ways to attract a loved one's attention. Coins are used in a general way as an object that can be seen and appreciated by many.

We have used this method since the beginning of time in order to grasp the attention of the living loved one in order to set forth the sign from the deceased.

In most cultures and societies, coins are revered, and therefore are sought after. The use of them became highly popular throughout history, and the highest incident rate of accepting of a sign became obvious. This type of sign can be used more than once, and in doing so reinforces the original sign.

As the appearance of new coins occurs, the sign takes on a more powerful connection. People understand that their loved ones, and even their guides, are around them even when they're not thinking of them. Often just thinking of a loved one will create the opportunity for the finding of the coin.

There are many methods we can use while placing coins in the path of the living loved one. Sometimes we will use the same denomination as in previous signs, so that the living loved one recognizes a pattern.

Sometimes the value of the coin will supersede the ability for one to accept the sign. They will notice the coin, but will immediately think of its value and not the possibility of the sign from a deceased loved one. This is often the case with those who are unaware of this method of communication.

People who understand this method in this manner soon realize that multiple signs are given using this type of communication. And each succeeding coin that is found is soon realized as a special sign from a loved one.

At times Joe, we have been asked to send signs in the form

of coins to many individuals at one time. This can be accomplished in a group setting where money is often distributed as part of an organized event.

It is also done at times when there is a great need for a sign by those who are asking for it. During these times, special attention is paid to where the object will be placed so that it is not mistaken as being placed there from another source. At these times, people will try to analyze how the coin could've appeared in that particular spot at that particular time. Often, they will come to the realization that it has been sent from another dimension.

We have asked many times that people send thanks to their loved ones upon finding such a coin. It lets their loved one know that they are sure that it has been accepted in the manner that it was sent. That is with love.

Sometimes we ask that others send out signals so that we may respond in kind with the materialization of such coins. By this we mean it is easier for us to send a sign such as this if the one in particular asking for it is willing to accept this particular manner.

At different times in your history we have used this method in various different ways. In this day and age, you find it quite humorous to find a standalone coin in a place that you had not expected it. In the past, people of certain cultures who found such a coin believed it had mysterious powers and could be used to gain advantages over others.

When this happens, we would use this method selectively in order to control the outcome of the sign being sent. We did not want to give the method a different result than was the initial intention. So as cultures change and mature, the methods that we use will also change and mature. The coin used today may be a different object we use tomorrow.

But for now, this is a familiar object that will gain much attention in your society, and therefore we will continue to use it as a method to send a sign from your deceased loved one to you.

Hello

> *When my father died and also when my mother-in-law passed in 2008 ... both times we found pennies everywhere. One day, I just finished vacuuming the stairs to the second floor. I walked back down and there was a penny on the step. I picked it up. Then I went to go back up about hour later and another penny was on the step. This stuff happened all the time after their passing. Nice of them to say "Hello"!*
>
> **Deb**

Author's Comments

It's important to recognize a sign when it is sent. With coins, it can be an ongoing occurrence as the method has been tested throughout history. When you accept the sign, it will increase your chances of getting similar ones in the future.

Mom's Coins

Another most remarkable thing that happened, and that still to this day happens, is that whenever I am out somewhere I find a penny. I attribute that to the fact that I always ask Mom out loud to go with me whenever I go out, just as I used to do when she was here. And the fact that I always find a penny or sometimes pennies and other coins is that it is obviously her way of letting me know that she is right there with me.

To date, I have collected hundreds of pennies. I always log each one along with the date and what happened when I found the penny or coin, and have filled over four books with notes on that. This is ongoing, and it is because I was always very close to Mom (and still am) and she first used to find pennies whenever we walked together and she would give them to me.

Now she sends me those coins, which mean the world to me, and I am very happy to know she continues to be with me in spirit.

LANCE

Author's Comments

In this case, finding coins is of particular interest, as Lance always asks his mom to go out with him. The fact that when he was young they would walk together and she would find pennies and give them to him makes a perfect connection for this method. Not only has he accepted these signs, but logs them in a book and continues to accept the fact that his mom is still with him in spirit when he goes out.

Canadian Penny

Only fair to give you a little history about me and my dad, Earl. I was the middle girl and one of five. Apparently, I was the favored girl as expressed by Verleen Eldridge, the medium. My dad and I are both Leos and understood each other.

Dad passed away 15 years ago. I feel his presence around me in the form of pennies. Most people find pennies, but I find them 3-5 times per week. I have had positive validation that it is him more than once.

One day I was feeling very badly about a situation. I got a message to look down. I looked down on the ground and I saw a penny. I picked up the penny and saw that it was a Canadian penny and was dated 1999. My father was from Canada and died in 1999. I felt it was a validation that he was there to support me.

Another time, I was at a festival where there were performers and artists. My father loved fiddle music. This group was playing fiddle music (the kind he liked) and

I noticed that there were pennies scattered all along the central aisle (I mean there were 20 pennies) I took that to mean that he was happy that I was enjoying the fiddle music, and to let me know that he approved and was there.

I notice that I get the pennies when there is a situation that would make me think that dad would approve. He was a practical sort of guy and he knew that I was too. Hence the pennies, which he would know that I understood the value of money.

It is so thrilling to think that dad is there with me on my life journey giving me his approval/opinion even when I don't ask for it

Thank you, Joe, for writing this book and for validating the connection with loved ones passed on.

ANITA

Author's Comments

Anita is fortunate enough to have recognized her signs from the beginning and therefore, especially with coins, she still experiences this type of connection. She mentions that she has received validation more than once telling her that it is her dad. This validation can come from other mediums, friends who knew her dad, or even through the contact of dreams. But what is important is the fact that she makes the connection complete by accepting these signs, and the loving intentions behind them.

Pennies From Heaven

Pennies from heaven -- that's what I'm told. My son was killed in a hit-and-run accident while on his skateboard at the age of 17. My whole life came crashing down. I was angry at God, myself and the world. I no longer had faith, or even the will to want to go on.

I was given a reading by a medium and she validated every detail of that day and the days to follow, helping me to see there just may be life after death. She told me when I see pennies my son was sending a message to remind me he was still here. One rainy night, I couldn't pull myself together; I cried, yelled at God and my son for leaving me. I was sad, angry and begged for a sign that he was still here and could hear me.

As I got out of my car to run up the stairs in the rain, I saw a penny was in the mud. I kept going up the stairs and something told me -- there is your sign, go get that penny.

As I reached for it, I couldn't get it out. It was stuck in the mud. I pulled and wiggled and as I was about to give up, it came out of the mud. What I had was a penny bracelet.

After asking several people if it was theirs, no one claimed it. It was my penny from heaven. Every time I seem to misplace it, or it falls off my wrist, it continues to reappear in the oddest places at the right moments when I need to know my son is still here.

IN MEMORY OF NICHOLAS SILVA THOMAS

Author's Comments

Pennies are often used to send a sign that a loved one is around. In this case, it took "something told me" to turn her around and focus on the penny in the mud.

But once that connection was made, the actions she took showed how strong the loving connection had been made from the other side. Another interesting fact is that when she misplaces the bracelet it shows up in different places, like her son is making sure she doesn't lose it.

Or perhaps it's an ongoing sign being repeated. She thinks she is the one misplacing it, but actually her son is actively doing it and then gets her to find it again when she is in need of knowing her son is still around.

Use of Numbers

Channeled from Joes Guides

Joe, the concept of numbers in your society is very important to individuals as a whole. You see, these figures that you call numbers are used in your everyday life from scheduling your activities to understanding the concept of time on your plane.

So we tune into this concept, as it is a theme that is easily used to make contact with your side. You take great significance in these figures in calculating where you have been, where you are now, and where you will be in the future. Many times, your lives are actually in-sync with certain time references.

You schedule your playtime, your work time, and special occasions around particular dates, times and other occasions that are marked by a particular numeric symbol.

So it is easy for us to tap into this concept when we are trying to relay a sign, a message, from a particular loved one. For it is easier for you to make the connection between yourself and a particular loved one while using a specific number that would be associated with them.

People remember loved ones by certain dates and times that are associated with them.

Birthdates, special occasion dates, and even the date when a loved one has passed, are all used to connect the deceased with the living. These particular numbers would only be associated with a particular person, and therefore the living loved one would recognize it more than other random numbers.

People living on the Earth plane will remember certain numbers associated with their loved ones throughout their lifetime. Some people remember the first house address they lived at, while others remember wedding anniversary dates, or even perhaps the exact time of death of their loved one.

Numbers are so prevalent in your society that we have many options to draw your attention to a particular number that will relate to your deceased loved one. You are surrounded by numbers in your everyday life, so picking the right one at the right time would be a sign that a loved one may choose to send. Sometimes we can affect a particular series of numbers when one is expecting a sign, or looking for a sign. Other times, we will have the living loved one's attention diverted to a particular series of numbers, and thus create the sign.

An example of this is sometimes the numbers related to license plates, or even numbers related to anniversary dates that show up in a public place. Many times, this is a great way to send a sign to multiple people at the same time. If two particular family members are thinking about a deceased loved one, or perhaps it is around a particular situation that would remind them of the deceased loved one, then we can take their attention, divert it to something that they both can witness, and the use of a number is a convenient way for us to accomplish this.

Oftentimes, numbers and symbols are related to multiple subjects at the same time. Therefore we can actually create a sign for multiple different people using the same figures.

So a particular number or symbol on a license plate may symbolize a birthday to one person, but later on down the road it may signify an anniversary date of their wedding to someone else. This is an example how we can send multiple signs to multiple people using the same sign, in this case a series of numbers.

This method has been used for many years and even now becomes more common as more people realize this type of method. As you, Joe, share this information with others, they will also share this information with their friends. This makes it easier for us to use this method to send signs, as more people realize that it is an actual attempt to contact them and not a figment of their imagination.

We will continue to use this method; at times we will change it slightly in order for the sign to be received and accepted as easily as possible. In other cultures around the world, we use other symbols and other techniques that are similar to the numerical symbols we use in your culture.

Numbers have had a significant place in the history of man. The concept of time and history are all based on series of numbers to designate where they are placed in the timeline on the physical plane. We just happen to use numbers as a method to send a sign because it's so prevalent on your plane of existence.

So with this understanding, we hope that you're able to pick up the sign that your loved one is trying to send to you from the other side, and that you are more willing to accept the sign, as it has been picked out especially for you.

Numbers can also be used to attach significance to a certain event. Events such as 9/11 in America can be referenced also in sending a sign. For those loved ones who lost relatives on this particular day, the use of the 9/11 numerical numbers would be a sign from the deceased loved one that they are safe, happy, and with relatives and friends.

Other events such as earthquakes, fires and group passing dates can also be used to send signs to multiple people on the same day. Many times, when one has lost a loved one during a time of conflict, numbers associated with that particular conflict could be used to gain the attention of the living loved ones.

So the concept of numbers used as signs can be complex. We try to use whatever method will succeed in gaining the loved one's attention.

So if you see a number or symbol and think it is related to a loved one who has passed, it is. It's their way of saying "hello" to you in that brief period of time that they have grabbed your attention and sent you that sign.

Friday the 13th

Chase's fave day of the year is any month where Friday is the 13th! His baby girl, Lailah, was born on 11/13, which is the same as our address (1113 XXXXXX). So on this Friday the 13th, Erin and I were driving across the St. Claude Bridge into the Lower 9, where Chase spent a lot of time hanging out with friends and their families, especially helping them in post Hurricane Katrina recovery. Erin and I had just crossed over the bridge and what do we smell? Cannabis (he celebrated 4/20 every year too)!

We talk about Chase, his cannabis, and how he would totally be celebrating this Friday the 13th! We have a quick giggle, and low and behold, what do I see in front of us? A license plate on a car showing "RIP 628." Chase's birthday is 6/28!! I don't know how he does it, but his signs are BIZAM!!

IN MEMORY OF CHASE DENVER
LOVE, MAMA & ERIN

AUTHOR'S COMMENTS

This story, like a few others, could have been listed in several categories. Like the chapter on special occasions. However, I think it was important to see how he used numbers to get his sign across. The date was used as a natural draw for both

Chase and the family to begin the connection, and thus put the whole series of events in motion.

The coordination of energy, back and forth with the smell of cannabis strengthening the loving connection, enabled the ride to continue until its final destination, being right behind the car with the license plate sign.

The Clock Alarm

My uncle, who was in his 90's, became ill and was sick in the hospital for a few weeks. Dave and I visited him one early evening. He was incoherent, but I talked to him; we were very close. I kept in touch with my family members about his condition over the next week.

A few days later, I woke up at 4:44 a.m. when the clock alarm went off and I knew that he had passed. Something told me that my mother and father (his brother) had come to get him. It was one of those eeeery moments, ... especial since the clock alarm was not set or even on! Of course, we got the phone call early the next morning that he had passed. We were told sometime around 4:44.

Jean

Author's Comments

It is not unusual for those who pass over to make a sign

attempt at the time of passing to loved ones. They can actually visit friends and family in different locations at the same time. They are no longer restrained by the physical laws of this dimension.

So by manipulating the electrical process in the alarm clock, he was able to send the sign that he had made it, was still alive, and could continue to share his love with his family.

The Hawks

> *I do believe in signs. Last week, when I was at the cemetery and I was talking to my deceased brother and he sent 48 hawks that soared above me, then they just disappeared. I mean I counted them. It was crazy, I never in my life have seen that many hawks in one place, ever. The number he lived at, and I still do, is 48 Hawk St! THAT'S CRAZY !!!*
>
> *I was like:" Okay, Ryan. I hear you lil brother".*
>
> RICH

AUTHOR'S COMMENTS

When our loved ones want us to get a sign really badly, they can make it quite obvious, as in this case. It was to tell his brother that he could hear what he was saying, and that he was still there with him. And Ryan replied that he too could "hear" his lil brother's message, loud and clear!

Skeptic No More

So no one is any more a skeptic than I used to be, but some things just can't be ignored.

My mother passed away on February 2, 2000, Groundhog Day… My parents had a very loving relationship and a bond like no other. A few years had passed and my Dad needed to be cared for, so he came to live with me. I went to a psychic with a friend (the one and only time I ever did) not knowing what I was looking for, but was looking for something. I handed her a picture of my Mom and Dad. The first thing she said to me was "Why do I see the number 222?"… I answered with my mother passed on 2-2 of 2000. Makes sense. So to me when I see that number I think of her. I have to add that my parents always commented on the number 178; I honestly don't know why but that was "their number."

Okay, skip ahead to recently. My father suffered from Alzheimer's disease, amongst other things, and he was at the point where he needed to be put in a full nursing facility. It was honestly one of the most difficult things I have ever had to do, knowing he never wanted to be a burden or end up in a place like that. Throughout the entire transition, I kept seeing the numbers 222 and 178 in random places. He ended up being there for only two months, but it seemed like an eternity while it was going on. I found great comfort in seeing those numbers. When it got very close to the end, the number 222 came up more and more ... I would see it on license plates, billboards, advertisements, on a TV commercial .I was having a terrible time sleeping at night and more than once I would randomly wake up in the middle of the night, check the clock and it would be 2:22.

Watching my father worsen was at times just too much to bear, so I would question my mother and beg her to come and take him, as he deserved better. It got to the point where I thought that I was "looking" for signs and it was all in my head. Then I kept noticing the numbers 226; I would think,-oh well, close but not quite. I kept noticing it along with the 178. I had thought that it was definitely all in my head and I was just grasping. His health worsened, and I struggled with leaving his side on a daily basis. I had left him on a Saturday afternoon knowing his condition was grave. I struggled all night wondering if I should go back or not. I finally fell asleep and woke up the next day to a phone call that he was not good and I should get up there right away. As I drove to see him for what I knew was the last time I did not hit one red light ... I knew that wasn't a coincidence, and as I was praying that he would wait for me to get there, I realized that the date was 2/26 and that was what my mother was trying to tell me. Fortunately, I did get there to be with my Dad while he passed, and I thanked him for allowing that to happen. After I left, I was driving home, I stopped at a light and right in front of me on a license plate were the numbers 222 AND 178....

Fast forward to my father's funeral. My parents were very active in our local church when they lived here. When my mother passed, people made donations in her honor to the "memorial fund" at the church. Those donations are dedicated and recorded in a book that is displayed in the back of our church in a locked wooden case with a glass cover so you can see it. My mother had passed 12 years prior. As I was getting ready to leave the church that day, I glanced at that book and it was open to the page with my mother's name on it ... I asked the people that worked there if they had done that on purpose, and no one had anything to do with it?

As I said in the beginning ... some things just can't be ignored.

In memory of Mom & Dad
Carol

Author's Comments

From a skeptic to a believer through the use of signs. In Carol's case, she was able to put the pieces together, and when she did, they made that loving connection so strong that the numerical signs began to show up more often as she was going through a most difficult time in her life.

Her mother was letting her know that she was there for her,

and was ready to meet up with her husband very shortly. They even gave a clue to Carol of the date of passing. When I say "They" I mean the mother and the father. You see, when someone begins the process of transition from a disease like Alzheimer's, they actually begin to cross over before they physically die. I have witnessed this in hospice situations, as well as in my Mediumship work. It feels like they're here, then over there, then back on this side, then back over again.

So they are actually in true transition during these afflictions. So with the date of passing Carol received, it was probably sent by her Dad with her mom's help to make the existing connection even stronger.

When signs such as these are presented, they are so strong that even prior skeptics will open their hearts to the obvious and begin to enjoy the loving bond that has been created between our side and theirs.

Use of Feathers

Channeled from Joes Guides

The reason we use feathers to connect you to your loved one is because they're readily available and they're easily distinguishable among other objects, and they have a history of being associated with the afterlife.

Some people think it's a coincidence when they find feathers in their path or among their personal belongings. We try to make it as obvious as possible when using this method for you to rule out all other causes except that it is truly a sign from a deceased loved one.

Often times we will use various different types of objects, in some cases various different types of feathers.

Some feathers may be small and appropriate for the space for which we have to work with. At other times we may use a larger feather in order to gain your attention. It is not the size of the feather that equals the size of the message. It just depends on the environment that you're currently in and the state of your emotional focus. By this we mean, if your mind is very busy and needs a larger object to gain your attention, we may use multiple feathers or ones of different sizes.

Throughout history we have used this method because it has achieved a high percentage of results.

During modern times, it continues to gain the attention of the living loved one, so we continue to use this method. However, different techniques have changed over the years. Sometimes the feathers in the past have been related to the environment, such as farm life and life in villages.

At other times, a feather would be inappropriate, as another method such as sound would work better in getting your attention.

But feathers are understood by many as being associated with a message from the other side. At times, people have associated feathers with angels. This is significant because the connection between the object and the afterlife has already been built into this particular object. Your history concerning the afterlife and angels makes it much easier for us to continue to use feathers in our attempt to contact you.

Some may associate feathers with angels to the degree they believe that an angel has actually left a part of themselves to the receiver. In essence, this is true to the extent that the message did come from a divine source and was manufactured due to their particular intention. However, it is not the actual physical piece of a divine being.

When a loved one decides to use a feather as the method for contact, they realize that their loved one has a high degree of accepting that sign for what it was meant to be. However some people will not make the connection, and will think the feather is just part of their environment. At times they will be correct, but most often when the feather seems to appear at a particular time or place that is not usual for that object then you can be assured that it is from a divine source. So accepting a feather or group of feathers as a sign from the other side is easy to distinguish from everyday objects associated with animals on your plane.

Feathers can also be used to contact many different cultures, similar to what we do with coins. There seems to be a universal acceptance of this method, so we are able to use this throughout the lifetime of the living loved one.

Don't be discouraged if a feather does not fall in your path, for there is a reason for this. We may have chosen a different method to contact you and reserved the presentation of a feather for either another time or different location.

It is true that some people are more accepting of the signs signified with the finding of the feather. In this case, we continue to use this method to reinforce what the loved one has already accepted as being a sign from the afterlife. When we say afterlife in this tense, we mean the spiritual realm which your loved ones have returned to.

We enjoy sending signs that people accept readily and are proud to share them with those around them. Usually people associated with feathers begin to collect them and even display them as a show to others that they're in direct contact with their guides and loved ones. Often times, one of your guides or teachers wants to let you know that they are still around you and working with you, and thus they will want to send you a sign.

So you may be working with this particular teacher or guide at this time, or they may be helping you on various issues that are affecting your life. This would be a wonderful method for them to gain your attention, as you already accept the fact that a falling feather landing in your presence from an unknown source is truly contact from our side.

We understand at times it may be confusing if this is a true sign, or if one is trying to grasp at any method in order to believe that contact is being made. We understand the enthusiasm some people may have in order to try to force a contact with our side. We work with these individuals in a different manner, as sending a sign through many of the current obvious methods cannot be done. For the individual to distinguish between the sign and what is happening in their environment is nearly impossible. They will be assuming signs are being received at the wrong times and during the wrong states of their emotions. By trying to force the acceptance of a sign, they will actually cause a disruption in the communication process.

We will talk about the methods we use for those particular persons in another chapter. But for now, we wish to let you know that feathers are one of our most common methods of contacting you.

We want to let you know that the method of sending a feather is only one of the ways we try to contact you. We do not wish to shock or disturb a person who may be in mourning with an obvious sign that might create confusion for them. With the feather, it seems this particular method is more relaxing and nonintrusive to certain people. It can be accepted or denied as easily as it is noticed. It may be a brief hello, or it can be the size of a shout. In this case, multiple feathers, or very large feathers, will be used.

Many times when feathers are used people may not understand what we are trying to communicate. We wish to let them know that we are trying to send you a sign stating basically you are not alone, your loved ones are with you and we are looking over you and taking care of you. This does not mean we're interacting in your life at that particular moment, or changing some of the life lessons you may be going through. It basically means we hear your prayers and thoughts and just want to let you know that we are in your presence.

Some people may call certain divine being angels; we call them guides and teachers. There are different levels of their divine inspiration and abilities. Some may be associated with healing, strength or even the ability to interact with actions that are taking place on the Earth plane.

This particular subject is very complex and for us to try to make you understand the concepts and differences between angelic beings, guides and teachers would be too much to add to this particular book and take away from the theme that we are trying to present.

A feather is also a way of thanking you for accepting the experiences that you have agreed to, being on the Earth plane. It is our way of connecting with you to let you know that we have not forgotten about you and what trials and tribulations you have agreed to accomplish during your life.

So a feather can have different meanings depending on the situations in your life. They can be a sign from your loved one simply stating that they are still with you throughout your life, or perhaps a thank you from guides and teachers who have worked with you in the past.

Do take the communication with the intent that it was sent, which is love. When you see a feather appear before you and you realize that it could not have come from any natural source, give a smile and open your heart and let the love flow between your plane and ours.

Moms Feather

> *I was sitting beside my mother in a hospital room. She had been in a coma for several hours and was unconscious. On the other side of the bed was a window with the curtain pulled open. Through this window I noticed a beautiful large white feather drift down from above.*
>
> *A few seconds later, I noticed this same feather ascend*

on an updraft. I then noticed that mother had passed.

CHARLIE PICKERING

Pet Sign

A couple of years ago, I had just finished reading a book about deceased animal communications with their owners from the afterlife. I began wondering why I had not experienced some sort of contact with my totally beloved Shady, who died suddenly in April 2010. I decided to pray to the universe for a sign that he was now alive in the afterlife. I did this for several minutes with all the intensity I could muster. I did get a sign!

About 2 weeks later, I was getting in my car after walking my two Shelties in the park when I saw a white feather stuck to the very center of my driver's side door. My car was clean and I had not driven in wet weather for a stray feather to somehow fly up from the street and stick on the door.

And you see, this is not my first white feather sign. I have had several, including during the passing of my mother. I still receive signs from the other side, and they often seem to be connected to a white feather.

CHARLIE PICKERING

AUTHOR'S COMMENT

It is important for people to know their pets also cross over and the love they shared on the Earth plane remains constant, even though their physical death has occurred. In this case, Charlie has had previous experiences with white feathers as a method of a sign. Often, they will use the same type of sign to communicate further contact as it is already recognized and will be easily accepted in the future.

The Bus

I've always had feathers come out of nowhere and fall at my feet. I just took it as a sign that my deceased loved ones and guides were always around me and just wanted to let me know they were still there.

Last spring, I was taking a shuttle bus back to the airport terminal after dropping off my rental car. The bus was packed with people as they always do to save time in shuttling people back and forth from the rental counters. I started to get a little anxious with that many people stuffed into the bus. At times, I don't really do too well in crowded areas.

So I started to try to talk myself into a calm state. I was having a difficult time when I noticed this single beautiful feather floating down the center of the isle. I was amazed as I watched this feather continue down the aisle and then suddenly stop and land right on top of my shoes.

I immediately knew it was a sign that I was not alone

and became immediately relaxed. It's amazing the unseen support that we all have.

K.J.

Author's Comments

A sign, such as in this case a feather, cannot only be used to show a connection of a loved one being around us, but also to show that we are being supported in a time of need.

K.J. was familiar with past experiences with this particular method, so it was appropriate that when he needed help with his anxiety that they would use this same sign to communicate that they were there too.

Knowing this helped him immediately, because he allowed his spirit to see the bigger picture of life: That we always have helpers looking after us on the other side.

The Interview

Often while writing a new book I come into contact with people who want to know what my latest project is. Recently, I was engaged in a conversation concerning the topic of Signs for this book, and I was asked to give an interview on a local cable TV show.

While it is difficult sometimes to do an interview on a book that hasn't been fully written, I had been far enough along that I was comfortable with giving examples and stories from this book.

During the interview, we talked about the concept of Signs in a general way and how this book relates to my first book Hello… Anyone Home? A guide on how our deceased loved ones try to contact us through the use of signs. I had mentioned that I was adding a few more common signs and stories that people could relate to, and why these methods are used by the other side.

After discussing a few different methods such as coins, numbers and feathers, the two people that were interviewing me kept coming back to the subject of feathers. They had both had instances where they had received signs from deceased loved ones through the use of a feather.

One of the interviewers, Josie, who had a son who passed into spirit several years ago, told her story about how she finds purple feathers when she's thinking about her son, Justin. She mentioned that Justin had a toy feathered bird when he was younger that was purple. One day, Josie was cleaning out the house and wanted to get rid of the bird, since Justin was now much older and they were going to have a yard sale. Justin took the bird from his mother's hands and said "mom I want to keep this one." She asked why, and he responded he just loved the crazy color of the feathers.

So it is appropriate that the feathers Josie finds

whenever she's thinking of her son are purple in nature. We all laughed at this story because who finds purple feathers?

The other person that interviewed me mention how he had witnessed the appearance of peacock feathers on several occasions, including once when one directly landed on his head. He mentioned there were no peacocks anywhere near his location at the time of the events.

So we had lots of fun talking about how they dropped a peacock feather on Ken's head, and about Josie finding her purple feathers, as well as exchanging other stories concerning other methods they used to send signs.

After the show was over, a few people in the studio came up to me and began to tell me their experiences with finding feathers, coins and other instances of receiving signs from the deceased loved ones.

I gathered up my things and was saying my final goodbyes in the entrance hallway with about a half-dozen people. As I started to leave, I turn to everyone and said: "Watch this. I'm probably going to find a feather today." And then laughingly I said I would probably find it in my car, trying to pick the most unlikely place one would appear. We all laughed and I waved goodbye and walked through the exit doors. I had not taken one full step when I noticed a beautiful white feather at my feet. As I was exiting the door, I was looking down as one might do to see if there was a drop-off so my attention was facing the ground. But there it was right in front of my foot just outside the studio's doors. I reached down and picked it up and had the biggest smile on my face as I knew then that all my guides and teachers were with me during this interview, as well as being with me at all times.

I immediately turned and stood in front of the glass windows of the door. I held up the feather with a big grin on my face until someone in the entrance way notice me standing there. They must've called out to the others because everyone turned around at that point and were looking at me. Someone reached for the door to let me back in and I was greeted with smiles and laughter as someone said it didn't take long. They all shook their heads and were amazed at how fast I had received a sign after saying that I was probably going to find one.

You see that particular method has never been used with me. This was the first feather that I had ever found. This is a great example of someone receiving a sign and being able to share it with others who understand the significance of that sign and will pass on the events of that day for years to come.

Since that day, I have found two additional feathers within one week. The last being when I reached into *my pocket to grab my car keys. A penny came out at the same time and landed on the ground. As I reached down to retrieve this penny, I noticed it had landed on top of a feather.*

The sign was especially powerful, as I had just finished the chapter on how they use coins to gain our attention. So a penny and a feather at the same time brought a great smile to my face, and a big thank you to all those who are working with me on the other side.

JOE HIGGINS

Use of Special Occasions

Channeled from Joes Guides

Joe, the use of special occasions such as anniversaries, birthdays and even the days when people pass over to our side are used mainly due to the fact that their associated with the deceased loved one. By this we mean there is already a natural connection between the living and the deceased. These common associated occasions are a natural link which makes the use of this method extraordinarily powerful.

When a loved one passes over and the method is chosen on how a sign will be sent back to their living loved ones one of the first methods we look at is the association with particular dates. These dates are a reminder to the living loved one of the specific connection to the deceased. When a deceased loved ones birthday occurs on your plane your thoughts and memories are immediately associated with the one who has passed. You are already open and willing to accept the sign even if it's just on the subconscious level.

So is a great time for us to take advantage of this particular moment as giving a sign has a greater chance of being received and accepted during this period.

Many times people ask for sign around a birthday or other occasions to let them know that their loved one is still in their life. At times, some of these signs are more easily accepted than if sent during other times of the year.

Special occasions such as weddings, funerals and other family get-togethers are also very good occasions for sending signs from our side to yours. During these occasions, once again the living loved ones think fondly of the deceased loved one and wish that they could be there to enjoy or share the occasion and gathering. This is also the main reason we use this method to try to send a sign. This gives us an opportunity to not only send individual signs to individual people, but also to send a group sign.

In this way, more than one individual will be able to receive a sign at one particular moment. It is our intention for more than one person to be able to receive a sign in order for them to discuss it with each other. When more than one person receives and accepts a sign from our side at one time and then discusses it with others who have also received a sign, it becomes more powerful. The act of sharing the sign with others binds the receivers together in a special moment. At that particular period in time, the receivers will be as close spiritually as one can get on the Earth plane.

Oftentimes, an individual will see a sign but be in doubt that it is really from the deceased loved one. Therefore they may not mention it, being in fear of being ridiculed. Some people may taunt them and tell them it's your imagination due to the special occasion or date. They themselves will doubt the sign as being wishful thinking due to the anniversary or special occasion.

This is one of the reasons why we would send a sign that is

seen by multiple people at the same time. If an individual came up to another individual and stated that they had witnessed the sign during the special occasion or date, the person who had the doubt may realize that the sign was of true nature.

Because, at times, reassurance from another is all that is needed for the individual to be able to accept the sign they had witnessed. So we afford this to that individual by sending a sign to more than one person.

Is very important to understand that your loved ones are still in your living lives throughout the learning and experiences you will be involved in until it's your time to pass. Many people fear that, once one dies, they no longer exist. [As I am writing this, I can hear laughter from spiritual entities surrounding the guide who is giving me this information, and I assume it has to do with the fact that some people think that once you die you no longer exist and they find that humorous] In actuality, you're more alive when you pass to our side than you are in the so-called living plane. Your reality is skewed due to limitations of your abilities to comprehend the existence of yourself on a spiritual level.

For those who pass over, we can still enjoy every occasion with you even though we are not physically on your plane of existence. Many times we would not be able to feel the excitement and sorrow as much as we can from this perspective, if we were still in a physical state. We look forward to many occasions in your life where you will celebrate your existence individually and with a group. Because we also get to enjoy that love and connection with all of you at a higher degree than you can currently imagine.

When the special occasions occur, such as marriages, perhaps a new baby arriving, and even smaller events such as a son's first baseball game or young girl's first love, we are still there for you. These are the times when the signs from our side become much more powerful, as they are associated with the special occasions. It is our opportunity to let you know that we witness these beautiful living situations from not only our side, but through the individual's feelings. We have the ability to actually feel how you are feeling at that particular moment.

There is a saying on your plane such as: "if you could only feel what I'm feeling now. " Well, on our side we can do that. So, the more energy around a certain occasion the easier it is for us to work with that energy and bring forth a sign about our presence.

In the past, we have found that using this method can bring great comfort to those associated with the event. The peace and healing associated with the sign at this time is magnified by the ability of the individual to accept the sign within the parameters of the event.

Signs sent on an ordinary day just to let you know we are still around and with you are special in themselves. But when we send a sign on a special occasion, it is more powerful because you have allowed yourself to be more open and willing to accept a sign. This is very important. Many times the sign will be sent and it will be received, but it doesn't always mean that it will be accepted. By this we mean someone can witnesses a sign, but have doubt about its origin. When one receives a sign during a special occasion, the threshold is lowered for the acceptance to occur.

Deep down, the individual taps into their true spiritual essence and allows the flow of energy to cross the barrier between our side to yours. Because during the special occasions, the essence of love is very strong. This essence of love opens up the communication channels much wider than during everyday life. With channels open wider and surrounded with love, the sign messages are much more easily transferred to your plane.

So when a special occasion comes along and you're thinking about your deceased loved one and wishing that they would there to share the occasion with you, just remember they are closer than you think. They stand by your side, they feel your happiness, they feel your sorrow and they are truly as close to you as you can imagine.So look for the signs during special occasions, because they will be sent from our side to your side, knowing that there's a high probability that you will be able to receive them and accept them from the loving source from where they have come.

Don't hesitate to share the sign that you have received with others around this particular occasion or date. It is important to share this information so that others may feel the presence of a loved one, even though they have not witnessed the original sign. Take advantage of sharing the sign and you will open up your ability to transfer love at a higher spiritual level while still on the Earth plane. This is an opportunity that is afforded to you, but only if you take advantage of it will you be able to experience the joy that comes with sharing such a loving spiritual event.

The Dress & Play Time

When my daughter Kristin got married ... I had something of my mom's to wear, jewelry and her pocketbook. But nothing from my mother-in-law. I looked through all her stuff, but nothing. It really bothered me, as we were very close.

The original dress I picked for the wedding got ruined just before the wedding. I was so upset and didn't know what I was going to do.

But the women at the dress shop said: "Don't worry; we can find you another one.".It was only a week before the wedding! I thought this is going to be impossible. I have so much to do, and now I don't even have a dress.

I went back to the dress shop and I tried on so many dresses. Nothing was working. I started to cry. The woman said: "I have only one more dress; let's try it".

I did and it was perfect!

I got home and the tag inside the dress caught my eye. JUNIE LEIGH ... was the name of the dress.

My mother-in-law's name is June and she lived on Leigh Street. It was perfect!!.

DEB

Kristin stayed at my house the night before her wedding. She woke up in the morning because she felt like she got hit with a pillow. She said this house has ghosts. I laughed, and I know it was papa (my dad). Because he always did things like that to her when she was little. They would sleep over and he would hit them with a pillow and wake them up ... Nice to know papa was at the wedding!

DEB

Author's Comments

Our loved ones don't miss weddings! They love the energy that surrounds such a joyous occasion. I've learned through my Mediumship that they actually look forward to such gatherings. In this case, they actually helped out with finding a new dress for Deb.

She also made the connection right away when her daughter mentioned that a ghost hit her with a pillow. So when you have that special occasion and you're missing a deceased loved one, don't worry, they are defiantly right there.

The Bell

My mom was born in 1921, and sadly passed away on December 23, 2010. Mom was an avid "bell" collector. Everyone brought her bells from whereever they traveled, and she proudly displayed each and every one in a beautiful collection around her home. She had about 200-300 bells.

When she passed away, we decided to share her bells with all our friends and family members who attended her funeral mass. During the mass, the priest asked everyone to ring their bells in honor of my mother. It was a beautiful moment I will never forget!

On December 23, 2011, I was at a "festivus" celebration; we were asked to bring a gift for a "Yankee swap." There were 52 people, most of whom were much younger than me, who brought wrapped gifts to the party.

The swap is kind of a game, as you have the option to "swap" the gift you receive with another gift that someone else has already opened. Lots of laughs and fun as people take away gifts from others they would rather have than the one they originally picked and unwrapped. I was number 22 and swapped the gift out that I had originally picked for a bottle of fine liquor.

I really wanted that bottle, so I was sort of hiding it under my coat!! When number 48 picked a gift, I didn't see what she had in the gift bag, but she kindly asked "where was the bottle of liquor picked earlier in the game?" Well, I had to give up the bottle and she handed me the gift bag. When I opened the bag, much to my surprise it was a bell!!

Exactly one year from my mother's passing, I was delighted Mom had sent me a sign in the form of a new bell.

JEAN

AUTHOR'S COMMENTS

This is another great story because it not only shows how a common object like a bell, that might not mean anything to others , can be so meaningful to one person that it can be used as a sign. But also that the delivery of that sign came on such an import anniversary.

The Anniversary Gift

On the Sunday of our 58th wedding anniversary, which for many years, in celebration of our anniversary, we have placed flowers on the altar at church, in memory of our parents. I did the same today, adding my late husband Murray's name.

Upon walking down the aisle, I saw the chair he always occupied, aisle seat, 3rd row from front, was covered in brilliant silver sparkles. It was the one and only chair covered in these sparkles.

As I sat in this chair, I realized the sparkles were placed to perfection, in diamond shapes, definitely heavenly made. I knew immediately this was an anniversary gift from my husband in heaven.

At the exchange of peace, I asked the lady sitting beside me "do you see what I see"? Her reply, "don't worry about it, if you were wearing a navy wool skirt, you would be covered in sparkles. You do not have any sparkles on you". I was wearing a new pair of navy cotton capris.

A friend noticed the one and only chair covered in these brilliant silver sparkles as she walked down the aisle to communion, and thought to herself, Betty Anne is enveloped in the universe today.

I later learned the custodian commented Thursday and again Friday she was having difficulty removing the silver sparkles from the one and only chair, and had no idea how they had appeared.

I phoned a Medium and asked for a private reading. On July 9th, my late husband acknowledged during the reading he had made this happen and said it was very difficult to do.

BETTY ANNE MILLAR
IN MEMORY OF MURRAY MILLAR

AUTHOR'S COMMENTS

Our loved ones often want us to know that they are still with us, especially on certain occasions. This being the anniversary of their wedding was a perfect time to send a sign to Betty Anne. Mr. Millar knew she would be at that location adding flowers to the altar that day, as they had done this every year, a tradition. Traditions are a great time to send a sign, as you're more open to receiving contact with your deceased loved one. So the brilliant sparkles on the chair, that specific chair, in a "diamond" shape would be the sign that their anniversary would be shared together once again. And a witness to this special occasion was provided through a friend who recognized the significance of the sign. This was so that Betty Anne had someone to discuss this memory with as the years went on. Every time pulling in her loving husband's energy when sharing this story, and thus making a new connection to him. There were many separate energies to coordinate: Betty Anne, her friend, the custodian and the woman sitting next to her, for this sign. And that is why Mr. Millar mentioned how difficult it was to make such a sign occur.

Use of Voices, Inflections & Thoughts

Channeled by Joe's guides

Joe, the use of a voice to make contact with your side is a technique we use on many occasions. These occasions will be to transfer a sign so that an individual will know that their loved one still exists and is still around them. Other times, we can use the sound of their voice to transfer information to an individual for further investigation and research. So this method is not strictly for the transference of signs from a deceased loved one to one on the Earth plane.

However, for the purpose of this example, we will try to keep the explanation of this method focused on the sending and receiving of a sign from our side to your side.

Often, people think that they hear their loved one's voice calling from another room or location. At times, this occurrence can be quite striking, and literally stops someone in their tracks. At other times, it can be quite jarring and cause discomfort and stress. This method must be used sparingly depending on the individual who is to receive a sign in the environment, and the emotional makeup of that person.

Often times, a voice may be described as something that is unrecognizable, but distinct. Meaning something that can be heard and understood, but also not recognizing from who it has come. When this happens, while we're trying to send a sign, we make a point of having the voice be as accurate as possible from the person who is sending it.

Each individual on the Earth plane has their own way of using their particular language. Even though the meaning of the statement may be similar, the way it is produced in an audible fashion may be significant enough to decipher between two individuals. Some of you may call this an inflection in one's speech, or others may accept this as just a personal trait of an individual.

Some people have certain phrases they use that their loved ones are familiar with, as well as the tone of the words they choose to speak. This inflection and tone is what many people understand and accept.

Usually, the first time that someone hears a voice that is not connected to any individual in the area, the living loved one pauses to decide if they wish to accept this particular sign. Often, they will rethink the audible sound that they just heard. Many will say it sounded just like … Often, the person will not remember what the voices actually said. So we try to make the messages as short as possible. Often, we will just use the name of the person receiving the sign.

Most people, when they experience the sign, contact friends and other family members to say that they heard their name being called. In this case, the sign has been received. If the individual goes on to tell the others that it sounded like one of their deceased loved ones, then the sign has been accepted. The sharing of the story, as well as all the stories of receiving signs, increase the chance that we use this method again, as others will be aware of it and they will realize they are not the first ones to experience this particular method.

Many times, when we use the voice of the deceased loved one, it gains immediate attention. By this, we mean someone does not need to be in a particular place or situation where activities have to be altered in order for the person to receive a sign. They can be going about their daily business and the voice can be propagated at any time and will grab their attention.

The main part of hearing someone's voice is that it's indisputable in its results. Once the person hears the familiar voice of a deceased loved one, there is no other explanation for the cause of this event.

With other methods of transferring signs, an individual might try to find other explanations for that particular event or sign. But with the voice recognition of the deceased loved one, there is little outside sources that can mimic such a sign. So when we use this method, it has to be during a specific situation which we feel it will have the best chance of being received, and thus the sign is accepted and remembered for many years to come.

Joe, you have been contacted by your mother in this method one day years ago. We know that while you're writing this information for your readers that this particular event has been brought back into memory. It is true that you tried to analyze the situation when it occurred. And the results of this questioning resulted in your acceptance that this voice could've come from no one else but you deceased mother. You heard her voice distinctly in a house that was empty except yourself, and reminded you of her past statements in that area.

The clarity of the inflection and tone in her voice was enough for you to stop the activity you were engaged in and walk around several rooms searching for an alternative source.

So it is proper that we inject your personal story here so that others can see that it happens more often than some would seem. We try not to use this method when there are many people around, or the participant may be distracted to the point where the voice would not be heard.

At times, the voice can only be heard inside of the loved one's mind. This is a more direct contact where more information may be transferred than a simple name. It is very similar to transferring information in the dream state. However, this particular method can transfer information to the individual while conscious.

Some people may be driving, in the garden or doing some other activity that has put them in the state of what you like to call daydreaming. The ability to participate in an activity while the mind wanders and thinks of other things. This would be an ideal time to activate the method of an audible voice.

We sometimes hesitate using this method, as some individuals find it disturbing and stressful to the point that it supersedes the importance of the sign being sent. We never wish to bring harm or distress to any individuals.

So we will back off and not use this method with some individuals because of the way they may receive it. We have many other methods of sending a sign to your side that we would begin to utilize in this case.

Do not be frightened if you hear the voice of the deceased loved one. It is only them, with the assistance of their guides and teachers, trying to contact you to let you know they're still in your lives, still in existence and that their love for you is still present.

Inflection

> *I experienced a very, very short contact the morning after my mother died of colon cancer. Here it is:*
>
> *Early in the morning, following the day my mother died, while still asleep, I heard her voice, crystal clear in my mind. She simply said "goodbye". But she said it with an inflection in her voice that seemed to be asking her guide: "Am I doing this right?"*
>
> **CHARLIE PICKERING**

Author's Comment

When one passes over and first learns to connect back to our side, they have to be taught the correct way of communicating. Their teachers are there to help them with this new form of communication. In this case, Charlie actually picked up on the inflection of his mother's voice as she made sure she was communicating the right way. Many times, they become excited knowing they have made contact and that the process of communication works.

Mom's Voice

> The most profound experience I have had by far after my mother's passing is that a few months after she was gone I started hearing her call my name. It is a nickname known only to her. It was unequivocally and unmistakably her voice. Sometimes I would be sitting at my computer working on something and I would hear her call me. Her voice was very strong and vibrant. Whenever I heard her calling me, the energy seemed to change around me and in my head. This occurred for quite a period of time after she passed. Sometimes I would hear her calling me very clearly several times a day and still do.
>
> **Lance**

Author's Comments

We see here that a sign can become repetitive when it is

successful. In Lance's case, the mother has perfected the audio method of using her voice to make contact. But it's just not the mother. Lance has to be able to receive it, and therefore he has also learned, subconsciously, how to tune the voice in. This make for a continued avenue of contact.

Asked in a Letter

My life-partner, George Miller, contacted me and most of his friends after his transition, and continues to communicate with me. I'll just tell you here of a few of the early communications with me. A friend had taken photos of me and my life partner some time before, and I was told he gave the negatives to my partner. He asked me to find them, as he wanted more prints made. I looked through a box where we kept all our negatives, but they weren't there. I had started writing posthumous letters to my life-partner knowing he could read them, and I added a P.S. saying if this friend had given him the negatives, could he tell me where he'd put them, as I couldn't find them. Next day I was standing in the kitchen and the words came into my head that they were on the top shelf of the larder. I thought this highly unlikely, but when I climbed up on a chair there they were, in an envelope, the two negatives my friend had given my partner without my knowledge.

After a few months writing these letters, I wrote that perhaps I should stop writing them so we could both move on. Next day, I got the urge to pull out one of his vinyl record albums at random and play a track without looking at the sleeve or the label. I was not very familiar with his record collection, as our musical tastes were different. He had a considerable collection of vinyl albums -- classical, pop, musicals, old fashioned songs, Scottish and Irish songs -- but I just pulled one LP out, having no idea what it was, and stuck it on the turntable, and put the stylus down on a track somewhere in the middle. Immediately my question of the night before was answered: Should I stop writing the letters? Dorothy Squires sung: 'Love letters straight from your heart keep us so near while apart'.

On our last holiday together in Jersey, Channel Islands, when my partner was very ill (he died a week after getting home), we were on a beach and he saw sand was getting into my cassette player. He knew I was coming back to the island next year with my mother, and made me promise to get a cover for the cassette player.

The next year, months after he'd transited, I was about to return to Jersey with my mother, but hadn't been able to find a cassette cover anywhere in the shops. I got another telepathic message while in my kitchen saying that I'd find what I was looking for in a cupboard where my partner put little things he'd bought or that people had given us which might come in useful for Christmas gifts, etc. I felt this was ridiculous; there was no cassette cover in there I was sure. There wasn't, but there was a little pouch for keeping valuables such as money or a wallet with a string to go around your neck. You wore it under your clothes. The cassette player just fitted into the pouch, and there was even a zip-up compartment which would hold spare batteries. He hadn't said I'd find a cassette cover in the cupboard, but that I'd find what I was looking for.

I'll end on a humorous note which gives a flavor of his sardonic sense of humor in life. In our 21 years together, he was never able to get me to appreciate classical music or opera, though he took me to some operas early on. After he transited, two friends wanted to go to the Coliseum theater in London to see 'La Boheme', so I went with them. I was moved to tears by the opera, especially the scene where Mimi dies. It has so many parallels with the hours leading up to my partner's transition.

However my tears turned to audible laughter when, as we left the theater, the telepathic message came into my head: 'I had to f***king die to get you to appreciate opera!' The message was so clear, I told my two friends, one of whom at least is a complete skeptic. I didn't care what they thought, my partner-in-Spirit, as I now refer to him, had spoken to me again and has continued to do so ever since. He transited nearly 23 years ago.

TONY PAPARD
LONDON, ENGLAND
IN MEMORY OF GEORGE MILLER

AUTHOR'S COMMENTS

Our deceased loved ones will use any method that will work to get their signs delivered. In these instances, a few thoughts were used at the appropriate time to get the signs through. Many times this method is reserved for the dream state, but for some individuals it can be used when fully conscious. The message about getting Tony to appreciate the opera was priceless and classic. They love to use humor, irony and their personalities when sending such a sign, as was used here.

Asked for Help

My boyfriend Rod lost his brother when Rod was in elementary school and his little brother, Jeffrey, was only 10. Rod was always mentioning that he wanted a gravestone rubbing of his little brother's headstone. So one week before Christmas, I went to the cemetery to see if I could find the headstone to get the rubbing for Rod. There was over a foot of snow on the ground, so with a shovel in hand, I headed down the aisle that I thought Jeffrey was buried in. I started to remove the snow for about 10 different plots and not one of them was the one I was looking for.

It was about 20 degrees out and I was soaking wet at this point. But I was determined to get this for Rod. I stood in the cemetery and said out loud, "Jeffrey, please help me here; help me find your headstone." Something told me to turn around and look behind me and about 15 feet away there was a tiny piece of a poinsettia left sticking out of the snow covered ground. I walked over and began to remove the snow from where the Christmas poinsettia was and, low and behold, I was at the right grave. I took a rubbing of the gravestone and thanked Jeffrey for his help. It was a nice Christmas as I was able to give the rubbing to Rod as a Christmas gift.

CINDI METRO

AUTHOR'S COMMENTS

This is an example of how we can ask for help and how they do listen. Cindi was open to receiving some sign to help her help a friend. She was not asking out of fun or curiosity, but out of desperation. And in this case, her plea for help was answered. Don't confuse this with asking for help in every situation. They do hear us, but at times are not allowed to intervene in the situation as it would change the lessons others may need to learn.

The Greeting Party

I would like to tell you about my experiences after my dear Mother's passing. A few weeks before her passing I started hearing what appeared to be voices coming from a square fan that was sitting on top of a chair in the living room. The voices suddenly manifested and would often be loud and sounded like there were many people all talking at the same time. This would occur only whenever I turned the fan on.

This continued throughout my Mother's illness until her passing. After her passing, I no longer heard the voices in the fan. I attribute those "voices" seeming to come out of the fan as being those from other deceased people who were making themselves known in this manner, perhaps as a prelude to what was to occur shortly with my Mom. And the fact they appeared as coming from the fan could be due to the fact that spirits need some sort of electromagnetic device with which to manifest themselves, and the fan apparently was the perfect venue for them to make themselves known. I have never forgotten this experience.

Lance

Author's comments

Often, before a loved one passes over there are instances of contact between the two sides. Especially after a long illness, the person close to death may experience visions and voices of loved ones from the other side. These are some of the people waiting to greet their loved one as they cross over.

In this case there seemed to be a group around Lance's mother before her transition that he was able to pick up. Sometimes these deceased loved ones are seen, heard or smelled by other living family members or hospice workers, thus ruling out medical hallucinations.

Use Of Shared Signs – Group

Channeled from Joe's Guides

Joe, there is a time when a sign is needed to be sent to many people all at once. The reason we do this is so many people can understand what we are trying to get across. The reasons are varied depending on the situation, and we will touch more on that in a minute. Sometimes individual sign connections are more important to the person who's receiving them. At other times, groups are used in order to magnify the sign. By magnifying the sign, more people are able to understand, learn and appreciate the sign.

As to the how, it's a matter of tapping into the subconscious of each individual and syncing them up together into one wave of thought. It is similar on your plane to a loud noise attracting the attention of many strangers. A foghorn may alert sailors on the water, but also those on the coastline. The meaning might be similar, but more acute for the sailor then someone safe on the shore.

When a sign is given to many people at once, we will use the abilities of everyone to recognize that particular sign. All those who are included will be connected in one particular subject matter. For instance, if we wish to send a sign on safety we could use a group of automotive specialists, or perhaps a driving school.

Sometimes signs are sent as a warning, as if a particular event will occur. This has been done in the past to groups of people regarding naturally occurring events on your plane. Animals are much more in tune to nature and can themselves create warning systems which are communicated throughout their community. We might put the thought or concern into several peoples' conscious thinking mind concerning a particular situation, and they will use these thoughts to share and spread the information that is necessary. So a black cloud to one person may mean a brief shower, but to another may be a sign of a change in a particular weather pattern. Those who have more knowledge about particular things, such as meteorologists or those who have experiences in the past concerning certain events, will be more able to help than others who are preoccupied with other things in their life.Sometimes signs are very simple, such as the flash of a light, the sound of a crash, or the whisper of thoughts of oncoming doom.

Joe, we can connect with many over a large geographical area if it is necessary in order to send a sign that is understood by the majority who receive it. We can help people focus on the certain situation that otherwise they may just observe and just let go.

By manipulating the communication centers of all involved, a sign is released, and hopefully is accepted for the reason it has been sent.

The reason why we send signs to so many at once is that it's easier for us to get the information across to those who need it most at one time. At times, it is needed to signal a group greater than one in order to get this information delivered. Sometimes, one individual may or may not understand the sign, while with a group the chances of successful acceptance is greater due to the amount of people that will witness it.

Many times the signs are given to groups of people concerning something they have in common. They can be weather-related, family-related, work-related, even social-related.

Different signs to many people could create confusion, so it is best at times to send one sign to a group in order for the misunderstanding to be limited.

These signs can be as easily transferred as a thought, an action or the ability to understand a particular event. It may be difficult to understand in theory what we are trying to say, so we will try to give you some examples of how this works.

We have discussed weather situations already, but in addition to that, we could send a sign to a group letting them know that their loved one is still around. This sign may be sent during a special service concerning the passing of the loved one. In this example, the group would all understand what the sign is trying to convey. Many times, people will interact and talk about the sign that they have witnessed and how it is related to the events that are going on at that time. An example of this is when people may relate that they understood a particular sign to mean a connection has been made to a deceased loved one, and that they understood this and affirming this information to see if others understood it as well, or perhaps just to signify that they are one more of a larger group who is received and understanding the sign.

Other times, signs are sent to groups to let them know that each individual is always connected to groups on your plane and on our plane. A sign might be sent to a particular social organization from others who have passed and were associated with that particular social organization while they lived on the Earth plane.

If, for example, a past president of an Elks Lodge, or perhaps another fraternal organization, wanted to send a sign to many members at once, he would have this opportunity to interact with the group as a whole as opposed to one or two individuals. By interacting with a group, the deceased is showing his connection not only to individuals but to the organization itself. It shows the bonds that were created in a group setting on the Earth plane can be transferred to the afterlife.

Joe, it's important to understand that an individual sending a sign to a group can be quite powerful, in that the group as a whole will accept it and strengthen the unity that the organization has already built on. It can be very powerful to be part of an organization that is recognized by a deceased member. By doing so, the member is recognizing the organization. They might also send a sign to individuals for personal reasons. But by sending it to the group, they are trying to inform the members that they are still there with them as part of the group.

Sometimes, deceased group members may like to play a practical joke on a group of fellow members. By doing this, the individual is able to bring laughter and healing to the whole group at one time. Many times, this deceased person would have had experience doing these types of things while living on the Earth plane.

The how is rather easy, as at most times a sign will be given when the group is together in one physical location, or during a brief period of time. This may occur over hours or a few days. The group may be involved in a certain pursuit over a short period of time, and this would allow a perfect opportunity for a sign to be sent and received by many, instead of multiple signs to individuals. Also, when many individuals receive the same sign, it enhances the power of it. These types of signs can be sent to as little as two individuals at the same time, as well as to hundreds celebrating a particular event or theme.

The standard sources of the sign can be used, such as the manipulation of electricity, sounds, music, or even the timing of a particular event. If the past president, or perhaps a past champion of a fishing club, wished to send a sign to his particular group, he may pick a particular tournament that the members will be participating in. He could help a junior member who lacks the experience and knowledge of catching fish to perhaps be aware of a certain area, timing, or gut instinct to catch a winning prize.

The members may laugh and acknowledge this deceased

member, saying such things as so-and-so would be so surprised, so and so would've gotten a kick out of this, or perhaps even "so-and-so is rolling over in his grave." But the main theme would have been completed, as the majority would have made the connection between this deceased member in the events that occurred that day.

These types of group signs are not limited to just social organizations; they are also used many times during religious services, including funerals, memorials and wreath laying ceremonies.

Sometimes these signs are shared with fellow family members during certain events such as holidays, weddings and other milestones that families share during their life.

Even if the sign is given to an individual and is understood, when that individual shares that story with others it then becomes a group message, a group sign. If something happens surrounding a particular event and a sign is accepted by an individual and they share it with others who are participating in this event, then it is a group sign too.

If a sign is to be sent to an individual to be passed on to a group, the individual is prepped by our side in order to receive and understand the sign. If a group is to receive and understand a sign as a whole, then the subject matter surrounding the sign will be more important so the larger group will have the opportunity to understand and make the connection. So to an individual, an individual meaning; to a group, a larger group meaning.

The more people who understand the connection that is made by the sending and receiving of signs, the easier it is to receive a sign, not only individually but on a group basis.

A Friend's Aunt

A few years ago, a friend of mine had lost her aunt after a brief illness. She was very close to this particular woman, as she had helped to raise her. She was like a second mother to my friend with all the joys and sorrows that go with being that close to another.

So when her aunt was ready to pass, it was a difficult time for her, but she realize that she was in pain and that with her age things were going to play out as nature intended. As I was witnessing this particular time in my friend's life, it reminded me of what I had gone through six months prior. I had lost my own aunt after a brief illness that summer.

My aunt was also like a second mother to me. I looked after her during her later years when she became less mobile. She was the last of her generation at the age of 89, having helped bury her whole family throughout the years. She often would take care of the family headstone in the local cemetery, having it cleaned and placing flowers beneath it on the many different occasions throughout the year.

The only relatives she had were her nieces and nephews. All lived out of town, and I was the closest to her throughout our lives. So I would visit her daily and spend some time with her. So when my friend's aunt passed over, it brought back memories of my own aunt passing.

The similarities between both our aunts were striking, as they both were very religious, both Irish and both had not ever married. So when I was attending the funeral, I felt like I was attending the funeral of my aunt again. After the funeral, my friend's aunt was to be placed in the family mausoleum a few towns over from where the funeral service had taken place.

So as the funeral procession paraded up the highway on a bright cold wintry day, it gave me time to think about all the wonderful things I had shared with my own aunt. As we arrived at the cemetery, we were given directions as to what particular side road we would take to get to the mausoleum. There had to be thirty or forty cars that began to fill up the side roads of this particular cemetery. But the funeral director and his assistants had done this many times before, and knew how to control the flow of cars in a densely laid out area.

We were probably the fifth or sixth car behind the vehicle that was carrying the casket. So as we pulled up to the mausoleum, we were told to wait in our cars until all the other cars had arrived at the cemetery. They also wanted us to wait so they could take care of the transfer of the casket into the mausoleum, and the fact that the grounds were covered with snow and it was very cold out.

As I sat in the front seat talking to my friend who had driven about her aunt, I could not get the thought of my aunt out of my mind. We had two other individuals in the back seat, and I was facing them and my friend as we waited for the funeral directors assistant to give us the signal that it was time to leave our cars and proceed up to the mausoleum.

Just before we were given notice to leave the cars, I had mentioned how my own aunt was on my mind and I could understand what the others in the car were feeling at that moment.

I turned to face the front of the car for a brief moment of inner silence before we were to exit the vehicle. As I turned to open the door of the car, I noticed I headstone directly in front of me.

The sight of this headstone brought tears to my heart and a smile to my face. Not only was this particular headstone the exact same size, shape and makeup of my own family's headstone thirty miles away, but the name engraved into the granite said "Higgins," my aunt's last name.

I turned to my friends and said my aunt is here with me, as I pointed to the stone. They were shocked that of all the cars in this cemetery the one we were in happened to stop right next to this particular headstone.

It is amazing how they can arrange such signs for all of us to share. In this case giving me serenity, and showing the others that life does continue and our loved ones will remain around us throughout our remaining years.

Joe Higgins

Winter Cardinal

I had a client whose son had passed, and when he's around, she would see a cardinal. I did a reading for her, and her son came through and mentioned that is one of the ways he lets her know he is still in his parents' lives.

One afternoon, on a cold snowy February, I was sitting at my desk looking out of the window. And there out of the blue a beautiful red cardinal flew up to my window and sat on the sill. Now, with all the snow all around, it was quite striking. Less than 30 seconds later, my phone rang and when I answered it, I recognized the voice immediately as the woman who had lost her son. She was calling me to set up an appointment to get some information about Medicare for one of her friends. I told her that right at this moment, I was looking out of the window at this beautiful cardinal. She started to cry and said that's my baby.

That was the first time I had talked to this woman in two years!

That's a great example of sending a sign to another to have passed along. The fact that I hadn't talked to this lady in two years, and she calls at the exact time that this beautiful cardinal shows up my windowsill, and that is the sign she receives when her son was around was just a perfect reminder to me how beautiful these connections can be. By the way, I'd never seen a cardinal land on my sill and it's never happen again.

Joe

Tree of Life

When Steve was dying - he was in the hospice at that time - I asked him to try and contact me when he crossed over so I knew he was okay. I also asked him to come up with a code so I knew it was him. He thought about it for a few days and then decided on "The Tree of Life" - it was a pendant/necklace he had given me for my birthday that year, which in and of itself is strange as Steve was never into that sort of thing.

The day after his funeral, my daughter and I went into

a local shop that sold incense, crystals, jewelry etc. The woman who owned the shop started talking to me and noticed my tree of life necklace. She said something to the effect: "it has been really strange. Over the last week, I have had quite a few people come into the shop asking if I had a tree of life pendant.". My daughter was with me and she just burst into tears.

A few weeks later, when my other daughter and I went to the funeral home to pick up Steve's ashes, we were faced with trying to pick out an urn to keep his ashes in until we were able to carry out his wishes. We stood there for ages looking at a wall of urns. The woman who was assisting us said after a while: "I have a few out the back; there is one there that I think you might like." We followed her to another room and there was a small glass-fronted corner cupboard. She picked one up and showed it to us saying: "it has the tree of life etched into it.". We were stunned and very emotional.

For a time - maybe six months - the tree of life came up in so many little ways. Both of our daughters have since had a small tree of life tattooed on their wrists as a tribute to their dad! So you can see how significant this experience has been in our lives.

Karren
In memory of Steve- Aspinall.

Author's Comments

This is a wonderful example of a shared sign. It even starts with the deceased deciding in advance on a particle "code." In this instance, "The Tree of Life" being chosen and then used to share his sign among the mother and both daughters on multiple occasions.

The power of the sign when shared among a family can be very comforting, as it acts like a bond between the deceased and his family as well as a bond between the remaining family members.

Five Way Calling

Twenty five years ago, my mom passed away. Four of her five kids were with her in the hospital as she passed. We were all very close to her in our own ways. Two of us strongly believed in signs and in the afterlife.

One week after her passing, we all lit candles in our respective homes. Three of us lived in New Jersey, one in New York state and one in Boston.

We were all thinking of her and sending a prayer at the exact hour that she passed away. Within three minutes, my phone rang, but there was no one on the other end. I remember calling one of my sisters shortly after, and hesitantly asking/telling her about the phone call.

Come to find out, all five of us had our phones ring with no one on the other end within three minutes of lighting the candles and saying the prayer! My mom's main source of communication had always been the phone. It just felt as though it was her way of telling us she was okay and safe on the other side.

In memory of
Katherine Craig

Author's Comments

This is a great example of a shared sign. The mother having the same sign delivered to each one of her children at the same time shows the strength of love shared between the family. They all participated in the lighting of the candles and prayers synchronized with the time of passing. This unison of activity made these signs possible, even to those who did not believe in signs before this event. It's interesting in that this particular sign was actually five separate signs to five separate people, unbeknownst to the others. But by sharing this gift with each other, the sign became a group sign to be shared among the children as a sacred bond between them, their siblings and their mom.

The White Flowers

My second experience was very unexpected, and very powerful. I have been a friend of Joe Higgins for quite a few years now, and although I am a realist, I have never doubted his abilities. That being said, one summer night in 2013 a bunch of friends had gathered at a local golf course for dinner and drinks. Myself and Joe were having a conversation about me feeling guilty about missing my Dad more than I missed my mom, and how I felt it was because I didn't have any time to say goodbye to him, and with my Mom I had 8 years to prepare. Joe was just listening very quietly and when I finished he said: "He wants me to give you this white flower." I said "What did you say?" And Joe repeated it, and I immediately started crying and Joe said: "It's your Dad and he told me to let you finish your story before I told you he was here." Joe said: "Why the white flower?" I told him that every year I was the one who took my father to buy all his flowers to plant. We would get about 20 flats of all different kinds, but as my Father began to lose his eyesight, the one flower that he loved the most, because he could see it the best, was a white marigold. He would drive me crazy to get it for him, because not every farm carried it and I would have to ask the guy from one farm to go to another farm just to get them for my dad! I would always harass him and say:" Dad, why white they are so boring " and he would say no they're beautiful! What a wonderful gift Joe gave me that night. I will never forget the feeling I had, and now I know for certain that there is life after death and I will see my loved ones again.

MARGIE

Author's Comments

I remember distinctly that night when Margie's father came through. The one thing with Mediumship is that you can remember readings/contact years ago like it just happened. I mean down to the details, including sights, smells, and the loving feeling I get to share as the deceased loved one shares their love with their loved one.

As a so-called go between, I get the residual love that happens when a connection is made. This loving connection was so strong that I began to cry. It was a very beautiful, special moment. He had placed our attention on each other that night, and didn't let anyone disturb us for the brief time we shared this connection.

This is another example of a shared sign, the white flower, that was shared with me and the story will be shared among family and friends for years to come.

Use of Personal Items

Channeled by Joe's Guides

Joe, the reason we like to use personal items as a communication method is that they are received more easily than some of the other methods. When one associates a personal item with the deceased loved one, the connection is much stronger than another method that can be used for many people.

An example of this is perhaps a watch, a piece of jewelry or something related to the deceased loved one that anyone else would not necessarily be connected to. A specific song may be associated with a specific love one, but a specific song can also be associated with many deceased loved ones. It is how it is used and when it is implemented that makes the difference when we use that particular method.

But with a personal item we can use that at any time. It doesn't have to be associated with a particular date or particular event or even a particular time. When a loved one makes the connection between the personal item the deceased has left behind, their awareness of this object will create a special energy between the two individuals that will cross over from the Earth plane to the spiritual realm.

Just having an object of the deceased loved one is not in itself a sign from our side. It is when the living loved one associates it with the deceased one that the energy opens up and the connection is made. We have the ability on our side to put the thought of the deceased loved one into the living loved one's mind, whether the personal item may be in sight or in proximity to the individual.

So an individual may come across personal items on a daily basis and not think anything of it. They were part of the possessions of the dearly departed and are associated with them, but the connection and energy has not transferred. This can occur while someone may be cleaning around the objects, or perhaps even transferring them into a safe location.

But as soon as the living loved one associates one of these objects with the memory, the thought of the deceased, or perhaps even emotional connection such as love with that person, then contact has been made.

We have the ability to materialize or move personal items to draw attention to them. At times, individuals on the Earth plane can be distracted by their daily lives. At times like this, when a sign needs to come through, we have the ability to gain the attention of that individual. Often, the individual may be stressed over certain problems or anxious over making a particular decision.

By sending a sign from the deceased loved one, it shows that they are there with them and trying to help them during their current situations. So at this time, we would make an effort to bring the individual's attention back to the deceased loved one in order to gain the extra strength, knowing that their love one is with them during this time of need. So objects that might not have drawn attention before can become the center of attention now. Many years may have passed, and the significance of certain objects may have dwindled in the eyes of the living loved one.

By us drawing attention to this object, it becomes re-energized with the loving bond between the two individuals. At times, the energy that resonates in a personal item can continue on even after the living loved one has passed over themselves. This energy around the subject is so ingrained with the emotion and love that it is not easily dissipated. At times, other family members who may not even have been born when the original owner of the item was living will feel this energy in this item, and the transfer of communications will begin again.

An example of this is perhaps the granddaughter having a special item belonging to her grandfather who passed over before she was born. The personal item can be used as a method to communicate a sign to the granddaughter even though her relationship to that particular item was not as particularly strong as perhaps her mother's.

We have the ability to transfer the association of the object from one generation to the next. By this we mean, perhaps the item had a specific meaning to the mother and a different meaning to the granddaughter. The same personal object can be used for a communication method, but a different energy is used for the transferring of the sign. The energy surrounding the granddaughter will be slightly altered from the energy that was used between the mother and her father.

Sometimes individuals who are not related to the personal item are also able to pick up the energy transfer between the living loved one and the deceased loved one. By holding a particular object of special significance, they may be able to comprehend who it belonged to or how it was used. The energy around the particular item will reveal its use and by whom. If the energy is very strong between the deceased and the individual the item was left with, then their energy too can be picked up. In case of the example above, a person may pick up the energy of the mother, as well as the grandfather, using the same special item. This does not happen all the time and cannot be done as easily as some individuals believe.

The object itself has no particular meaning; it is just used as a conduit between the living and the deceased. It is the energy that is associated with those two individuals that creates the connection. The third-party who holds a particular object and so-called "reads" the energy associated with it does not actually receive a sign themselves, but only the energy of the individual who is associated with that item.

We have used this method many times in the past, as people have a hard time letting things go that are associated with the deceased loved one. Some people in the past traveled, often over large distances, and believed if they carried something of the deceased loved one they were actually taking their loved ones with them on their journey. That is why many people keep small tokens of their deceased loved ones, as they are easier to store and transport than larger items.

Often, items that are associated with special occasions are also kept. However we do not use these particular items often, as they do not transmit the energy between the two individuals very well. An example of this may be a particular wedding gift that is received by a husband-and-wife. This object could be used for sending a sign. However it is likely that the sign would not be received and therefore the attempt is not made.

But a smaller, more individualized object such as a wedding ring would fit the parameters of a special item between the two individuals. This type of particular item would work very well in sending such a sign.

Remember it is not the actual object that is sending a sign to the living individual. It is the object that creates a thought about the deceased individual. And then the time that this thought is manufactured usually has a significant impact on the connection.

So if someone is thinking about the deceased loved one and they come across a specific item of that loved one, then the sign has occurred. The how, the makeup, of that sign is all worked into the appropriate time and the response that the living individual will have. It is our belief that when memories and thoughts of the deceased loved one are strong, or needed to help the living love one, a specific object is a great method to have that sign, not only recognized, but more importantly, accepted.

People need not worry if a special item belonging to a deceased loved one becomes misplaced, lost or forgotten. We have many other methods of communicating with your side and we will adapt to this situation. We do not want to bring stress or anxiety to loved ones due to the fact that a particular special item is no longer in their possession. There are reasons why this may have occurred, and they are complex in their makeup. We do not wish to try to explain this at this time, but we do want to mention it so as to relieve possible pain or stress with those who have confronted this situation.

Our love will find a way to connect with your side one way or the other. We have many assets at our disposal, and we will use the most efficient ones at the proper time.

The Rug

I had been feeling extremely lonely for my son, Chase Denver, as usual after his passing. As those of you know who go through it, the roller-coaster ride never ends.

Chase's sister, Erin, brought home a bed and other furniture someone was giving away. The bed will go in Chase's loft, and now I can finish decorating the loft.

Next is purchasing a new quilt for the bed. Found it!

Great colors with his fave, blue, that will tie in downstairs (Tuscan).

Erin's PTSD research appointments at Tulane Medical Center are Saturdays. We'd had our 5th visit in the same office. Today is the day I noticed the rug under my feet, while I'm reading her Kindle. I said: "OMG, this rug would go PERFECT with the quilt I bought for Chase's loft!" I'm so very excited about the colors being an exact match to the quilt that I tell Erin I'll look for a label on the rug to find a brand, UPC code, something so I can buy the rug. Well, don't you know, the rug is called JULIAN, which is Chase's last name! Can we get any clearer of a message from him?!!!

Thanks for the slap in the face, Chase. Erin & I were high-fiving!!!!!!!!!!!!!! I can hear Chase saying: "Ma, this stuff is fiyah [fire]!! You were right - I can get through to you anytime I want!!" Of course, I'm now trying to find this rug to purchase and put in Chase's loft.

SANDRA

Author's Comments

This is what I call a "wow' moment. A moment when the sign is so recognizable that it's like a slap in the face. As Sandra mentions, thanking Chase for the "slap-in-the-face" sign. Often, these types of signs are used to make sure there is no doubt about their connection to the deceased loved one.

She was redoing Chase's loft and he wanted her to know that he was part of that renovation and was helping out. It also involves his sister, to whom he was very close, thus causing a shared-sign event with his mom. So an unmistakable sign was called for in this instance and it work perfectly.

The Buffalo

> *I was making the bed and there was a thud sound in the other room. A carved, wooden buffalo that Mom brought us from Africa, which has sat on the high chest of drawers since 1973, had fallen. It was not close to the edge and no one else was home.*
>
> *It landed with all four legs standing on the carpet. I knew instantly it was a visit from heaven. Timed to perfection, as the limo is arriving to take me to the airport as I am attending the Academy for Spiritual and Consciousness Studies 38th Annual Conference in Phoenix.*
>
> BETTY ANNE MILLAR

Author's Comments

Many times, Spirit loved ones will move items to get our attention. These can be general in nature, meaning not associated with a particular object, but just to get us thinking. But in this case, the item was a gift from her deceased Mom and sent at a particular moment when it was appropriate to her understanding the meaning of the movement. She "instantly" made the connection, as it was intended.

The Beatles

Today, Erin was cleaning up her room, tidying and sorting clothes. She found her deceased brother Chase's brown Beatles T-shirt and put it on her bed, looking at it, and reflecting on Chase ... thinking of how much she misses him and wishes he were here. So she never thought anything of it at the moment ... she always misses him. Nothing new.

After cleaning up, she brought her dog, Luci, to the Battlefield (War of 1812 a/k/a Battle of New Orleans). I married Erin's daddy there. I've spent many, many hours there. Lots of great memories as a little girl myself, and with my kids. I used to bring Chase there to roll down the levees, sit on the river, and brought Erin to skip school one day to sit on the wall in the river. Great memories.

Anyway, Erin's been bringing Luci there a lot lately for evening runs. She feels as much of a connection to the place as Chase and I have. As she's walking down the main entrance to leave, she spots something on a bench ... something is white and draped. It caught her eye, so she went to see what it was ... lo & behold ... a brand new, white Beatles T-shirt ... in her size!! No one in the area knew where it came from, and they said it wasn't there a few minutes ago.

Once again ... Bobo comes through for his Munchkin. I'm beyond thankful and feeling blessed to have such a wonderful, caring, compassionate son. No matter that he's not here physically, the connection he has with Erin goes far beyond our physical realm.

I'm beginning to feel like these "signs" are miracles. Because they always come just when we are at our lowest points, missing him, talking to him, writing letters, poems, art ... most in memory of him.

I love you so much, Chase. And I love how much you love your little sister. Thank you doesn't seem to be enough.

Sandra
In Memory of Chase Denver
Love, Mama and Erin

Author's Comments

This is not as unusual as one may think. Often, things are left for a loved one to find in order to bridge that gap of physically not being there. In this case, when Erin wears the shirt she will feel her brother's as close to her as possible. This was his intention when she picked up his Beatles T-shirt that morning.

It's all planned out; we just need to put the pieces together. And sometimes they help with that too, like in this wonderful story.

Eternity

I would like to start this story off by saying that I am a realist by nature -- everything in my world is usually black and white, not a lot of gray area. I have heard many stories about people having spiritual experiences and have been somewhat skeptical, and have always said that for me personally to believe that a loved one was contacting me from the other side you would have to tell me something so personal that there would be no doubt! Something that no one else could possibly know.

With that being said, here is my story... It started in September of 2012 when I lost my Mom to Alzheimer's, a battle she braved for 8 years. Although I knew it was coming, it was devastating! My Dad was left in great despair, the love of his life for 64 years had left him and he let it be known to all of us that he wanted to go too. His life here on Earth was nothing without her. He always said that God had been so good to him in his life, and he prayed for God to take him to be with his beloved and once again God answered his prayers. Twenty five days after my Mom left this Earth, my Dad joined her!

Although I knew that's what he wanted I was crushed. I had only just begun to grieve my Mom, and now my Dad was gone too. It was inconceivable! I was in a fog, just going through the motions, a little angry with God for taking them both so close together. But at the same time, I knew that God answered my Dad's prayers, so how could I be angry at that. God has been good to my family in so many ways. So I had to keep my faith strong at the most difficult time in my life, and believe that it would pull me through.

After a couple weeks of grieving, I returned to work as a school crossing guard and as I would stand at my post I would pray. I would ask God to fill the hole in my heart and to somehow let me know that things would be OK. One morning I was standing at my post and, as I turned to leave, I noticed a pamphlet stuck in the one little bush that was next to me. Something made me lean down and pick it up, and it was from a church that I didn't know of in a nearby city and it said "Where will you spend Eternity?"

You could have knocked me over with a feather! My Dad always wore a black baseball cap with a red letter "E" on the front, and when asked what the "E" stood for he would always answer: "Eternity." That was a clear sign for me. I looked up towards heaven and said "OK God. Thank you ".

M. WHITE

Author's Comments

In this story, Margie is thankful for things that have happened in her life, but still reaches out for help in her grieving.

When she did this, it opened an invitation for her loved one to come through with a sign. While standing at her post, she said that she would pray, so it was decided that would be a perfect place for her to receive the help so has asked for. So they wanted to make the connection between her and her dad simple and direct. An item her dad wore all the time with his specific interpretation of the letter "E," and the pamphlet with Eternity written out.

That perfect loving connection, between father and daughter was picked up immediately by Margie, bringing comfort and thanks.

Multiple Methods

My husband died at the age of 33 while I was expecting our third child in an unexplainable single-vehicle accident. I buried him the day of our 9th wedding anniversary. I remember sitting in a chair in a daze, not believing what happened a few hours after he died when I suddenly realized something was in my hand. It was his little black comb. I jumped up and ran outside sobbing to look up into the sky to tell him I knew it was him telling me he was near and OK.

Now I find those combs and pennies in the most unlikely places.

I was in bed one night and I saw in front of me, like an old movie reel type film, Neil crouching at the edge of a river, his back to me. I wondered why and realized he had long hair at that moment.

He had cut 19 inches of his beautiful black native hair shortly before he died to be in a friend's wedding party, and he regretted it. I found the long braid of hair he had kept and put it in his casket.

He was showing me he had his long hair back! So many signs in the years to come, including a voice telling me "it's closer than you think!"

When I cried out, I know you're OK in heaven, but it's just so far away! He died August 10 2002.

On July 10 2012, our son suddenly joined him on the other side at the age of 16. Unknown natural causes, they tell me. I've heard him call "Mom!" to me. He left a handprint on my bathroom mirror.

He makes my shower head randomly spew water out when I'm crying in bed. He comes to my 10-year-old in dreams to simply say: "I'm OK!"

Dana Tate
In memory of;
Neil and my son Keiran

Author's Comments

Dana has shown that they can use many different methods to try to contact us. In her case, an object -- the combs -- as well as a voice from hearing her son say "Mom." Dreams are used here through a family member, her son, to bring through more information, in this case "I'm OK," to be passed on to her.

Often deceased loved ones will come through showing themselves as they wish to be seen. Healthy, and in this case, with his long hair intact. Many times, people who have lost their hair due to cancer will show themselves with their full head of hair.

Section IV

Other Examples of Signs

Don't worry about us; after we transition, focus on your life and how you can learn to love more.
J.M.H

Channeled by Joes Guides

Joe, what we would like to explain to your readers in this section is that we use a multitude of methods to gain your attention and therefore increase the chances that a sign will be accepted. We understand that people enjoy reading about others' experiences when it comes to receiving and accepting signs from their loved ones. It is important when people share these stories, for spreading this type of information will only increase the opportunities for others to also receive signs from our side.

Oftentimes, people are reluctant to mention a sign that they have received in fear of being laughed at, or even judged to be unfit. When people read stories that you have provided in this book, it increases the chance that this information will be spread to a wider audience -- and with this, the understanding that these contacts are not unusual in themselves, but are part of everyday life for people on the Earth plane.

As we have explained to you when we were helping you write your first book, Hello... Anyone Home?, the use of smells, dreams and sounds are easy methods for us to communicate with your side. As you have seen in some of the previous stories, we have the ability to manipulate electricity as well.

The methods we use are as varied as the intellectual makeup of every human being on the Earth plane. By this, we mean we will use whatever method resonates the best within a person's cognitive processing abilities. These abilities may shift and change over the course of one's life. So at one time in someone's life, we may use one method; but in a different time in someone's life, we may use another. This shift can be caused by grief, the aging process or the particular environment the individual is currently in.

There are also much more complex methods of us interacting with your plane of existence in order to communicate not only signs, but also information that loved ones can use to move along their path of existence in that dimension. An example of this would be putting a thought in someone's mind that may help them create a piece of music or art work. Perhaps it might be strength one may need at a particular time in their life in order to advance on the path that they have chosen before they were born.

Dreams

Mom's Message

I was 53 years old when I was told that I had Stage 2 breast cancer in December of 2009. My oldest niece was very close to my Mother who had passed away on her birthday, 7/9/2001. After my Mother's passing, she would come to my niece in her dreams talking to Shanie about the present day. After I was diagnosed, my niece called me one day to tell me that my Mom had again come to her in a dream. She said "Maw Maw told me to tell you that you are going to be okay, and to be strong." At that moment, I felt an overwhelming feeling of comfort come over me, and from then on, I wasn't as afraid as I had been with the diagnosis. I knew that my MOM was watching over me.

PATTY LUCIA

Author's Comments

In this contact we see the sign/message coming through a family member to be transferred to the person who it is intended for. The sign might not have been successful if it came directly to the mother, so they decided to send it through the niece, as she had a great relationship with Patty's mother.

Watching Over Me

My Dad passed away three years ago on Feb 16. I still

miss him every day. One night in April (not sure of the day) of the same year, I had a dream, and in the dream my Father came to me and said: "Tracy, I'm busy "up" here. I don't have time to keep coming to see you. But I need to tell you one thing: John's (my son) arm needs to be looked at. It needs attention."

The dream was so vivid, that as soon as I woke up the next day, I made a doctor's appointment for my son. Thankfully I did, because he had a bad problem in his shoulder and needed surgery. We were told that if we had not gone, he would have had life-long problems with it! He had told me it was bothering him a bit, but he is a baseball player so I thought it was normal 'wear and tear." I had no idea it was that bad. I thanked my father for coming to me and letting me know about my son!

My dad may be gone physically, but he is still watching over my family. Since then I have had numerous little things happen to me and I know it's my father, letting me know he is always with me, watching over me and my family. These moments bring me such peace, and help to take the hurt out of losing him. I believe it is the reason he keeps doing it!! I could talk all day about him, but that's just one story of many!!! Miss ya Dad!!!

Tracy
In memory of Thomas Tinkham

Author's Comments

Dreams are one of the easiest ways for our loved ones to contact us. We are relaxed and they have access to our memory and reality processing systems. When we get a warning about something like Tracy did with her son, it has been "approved" to be passed on to our side. Meaning that it was not a necessary learning lesson for him in the future. It could have been meant to be taken care of earlier, but Tracy was associating it with regular "wear and tear" of playing baseball, thus putting off the diagnosis. This is not to say that another event, possibly another injury, would not have exposed this problem later down the line. By having Tracy's dad come through to tell her of the issue not only saved his grandson the pain and hassle of having to experience another event in order to reveal the problem, but also provided the opportunity to connect with his daughter and let her know that he was truly watching over her and her family.

Smells

Grandad is Here

My story involves my brother, Adrian, and I. Have you ever noticed that if youenter the hallways of certain houses that you would visit in your lifetime that there is a strong distinct scent in the house? Not in all houses, but in some.

Anyway, about 6 years ago one Tuesday afternoon I was watching TV in my father's den. I suddenly got to smell a very strong scent in the room.

It was not there earlier. It was the same scent that one would smell when you enter the hallway of my Grandfather's house. He would be my father's father who passed away in 1983.

Anyway I recognized the scent as being from my Grandfather's hallway. As I recognized it, my brother, Adrian, walked into the den, stood behind me for 5 seconds and said "Grandad" is here." He got the scent as soon as he walked into the room.

It was amazing how the two of us got the scent at the same time and we both came to the same conclusion.

Roy Cleary
Republic of Ireland

Author's Comments

Here is a great example of a smell being used as a method of contact. It was recognized immediately by Roy as coming from his grandfather. They realized that he would associate that scent from his memory of his grandfather's house.

When Roy's brother, Adrian, also immediately recognized the smell, it now became a shared group sign. Thus the two of them sharing the same experience and being able to talk about it to each other reinforced the point that more than one person can receive the same sign at the same time.

Electricity

The Door Bell

My name is Graeme Jeffers. I am 73 years old and I live in Brisbane, Australia. The story I am going to relate to you here, happened some years back. I was watching James Van Praagh's show on TV one afternoon, when as the show was ending one of the audience members asked him how do people in the afterlife contact you. He stated some different ways, including ringing the front door bell. I said out aloud to my deceased mother, Mum if you're listening, ring the front door bell. But nothing happened.

The next day as his show was ending, again I thought of my Mum, this time the doorbell rang. When I went to answer it, there was no one there. It had to be Mum fulfilling my request from the day before. This is not the only experience I have had in my life. I am definitely a firm believer in life after death.

GRAEME JEFFERS

AUTHOR'S COMMENTS

The probable reason his mom did not answer the first day is because the request came through as a test. Like, "prove it to me." The next day, just by thinking about his "Mum," the request was fulfilled.

So be sure when you ask for a sign to do it sincerely and let it go. Don't put conditions on it or make it a test.

Phil's Cell

My Mom decided a couple of days after Phil passed accidentally that she would charge his cellphone so that she could go through it and call any of Phil's friends so she could to tell them that Phil had passed. On the second or third day after he passed, she heard his cellphone ringing up on top of the piano. She thought that was funny that it was ringing because Phil didn't have a ton of friends so she wasn't sure who would be calling. She picked up the phone and she just heard his voice mail saying "Phil xxxxxx" and then the call ended.

My Mom was so freaked out, she threw the phone across the room. Because the only way she would have gotten his voicemail would be if she had called the phone, then it would go into voicemail. But the fact that the phone was ringing and she picked it up and then heard Phil's voice in his voicemail message saying "Phil xxxxxx" and the call ended. She immediately called my sister to tell her, as my Mother was very upset over it. My sister reminded her that it was Phil trying to get in touch with my Mom and tell her he was okay.

DIANNE

Author's Comments

The use of a phone has been utilized for many years in the process of contact from our deceased loved ones. It seems that the electricity, or the power it generates, helps with this method. It is also a form of communication known to all of us, and thus known to the other side as associated with communications. If we could speak to our deceased loved one, a phone would be the perfect choice for most of us.

Wake Up!

In Hawaii one night, when I'd asked for a sign that my husband was there, I was awakened in the middle of the night by voices. Eventually I realized that a TV in a closed upper kitchen cabinet, a TV I didn't even know existed, was blaring CNN. It was located in a wall adjacent to my bedroom and the farthest wall from the other bedrooms in the house, so no one else was disturbed by it. This happened at roughly 3 a.m. Thanks for the answer!

JOAN KATHERINE CRAMER

Just Saying "Hi"

After my husband died I got a new cellphone. Periodically, for a year and a half, I have been getting calls on that phone for someone with my husband's first name.

JOAN KATHERINE CRAMER

Author's Comments

When Joan asked for a sign from her husband, she was inviting him in to make contact. We can invite people -- guides etc. -- in subconsciously too. So you should be aware of that. Joan's husband decided to send that sign at a time of day that it would not have been confused with everyday activities. The fact it was in a closed cabinet and did not disturb anyone else but her was validation that her husband had indeed made contact.

For years, spirit have used the phone as a method of contact, as it was something that got our attention immediately. So their methods have not changed, but just updated to the times with the use of cellphones.

Music

Mustang Sally

My Dad was an avid fan of the song "Mustang Sally." Seems he couldn't get enough of it. He would call WROR, the oldies station in Boston EVERY single day at noontime for the request hour and would request Mustang Sally ... it got to the point that the DJ would say live on the air sometimes, "oh no, not you again!" We used to laugh when he would tell us the story. So on Sept 21, 2001, I got the call at 2 am that my Dad was at the hospital and he had just passed away from a massive heart attack.

The next morning, my sister, brother and myself went to my stepmom's house with all my Dad's siblings and made all the plans for the funeral, etc. and sat and exchanged stories about Dad. I told his older siblings about his love of "Mustang Sally" and his daily call to the radio station. My sister and I left our stepmom's in the afternoon and once we hit Plymouth, we drove past the Public Library and they were having their annual book/yard sale, which we would go to every year. My sister looked at me and said, "wanna stop in?" I was game, as we had had such a sad morning and were all in a state of shock. My sister and I headed to the book section and she was down one end and I was at the other browsing books and the DJ had been playing CD music. We hadn't been there for 5 minutes when all of a sudden Mustang Sally started playing. My sister yelled down to me: "Are you hearing what I'm hearing?" and we both burst out crying. We put the books down and headed for the car, both of us in tears. We got into her car and she turned the car on and what was playing on the radio? (not a CD, the radio) but "Mustang Sally." My sister just looked at me and said: "This is definitely a sign from Dad that he is with us!" We were just speechless, and we still talk about it to this day! Just too much of a coincidence to brush it off. It even gives me goose bumps to talk about it today.

Dianne Metro Turner

Author's Comments

This is a perfect example of how our deceased loved ones use a particular song to gain our attention. It was of such importance that they would share the story even before the loved one had passed. So using this sign was a natural choice for making contact.

The sign was not only used once, but twice in a short time frame to reinforce any doubt that might have occurred later on. We also see that this sign was sent to two individuals at the same time.

This occurred not only because of the shared grief between two sisters, but also so that it would be shared with other family members and friends, thus bringing some healing and peace to others.

Multiple Signs

My husband of nearly 30 years passed away almost two and a half years ago. He was diagnosed with terminal stomach cancer in October 2011 and died 2nd December 2011. It was like a freight train bearing down on all of us. During his illness, there were a few significant occurrences.

Two weeks prior to his death, I kept waking up at 5.55 in the morning – I knew it was significant. On the morning of his death, he stirred at about 5.50 am. I said to him, it is just you and me here (something that was said often in which he would say "just the way I like it"). He then opened his eyes, looked over my right shoulder and then took his last breath.

The next morning after his death, as I woke I was still in that state of non-movement. I saw him walk past me, from the doorway, alongside my bed, and he kept going through the wall. He had a determined look on his face as though it was hard work and he wore clothes that I would have never imagined him in. Sort of like a safari suit outfit but made of really light material. I remember almost laughing and said: "You have to try harder with the clothes."

A week later as I fell asleep, I dreamed of him smiling at me through the screen door into the lounge room; this time he had on a broad brimmed hat and *flannelette shirt. I laughed again at what he was wearing. It seemed like a bit of a joke.*

Joe, I had to think for a while about this. When Steve was a teenager, his dad made him take his sister to her high school formal because she didn't have a date. His dad, who was English, had him made a safari suit -- still have a picture of him scowling in it. The safari suit was a bit of a sarcastic type of joke for many years. Also, he used to wear favorite clothes -- the ones he would just wear around the house or yard -- to death! One pair of favorite shorts he tied up with bailing twine to keep them up, as all of the elastic had gone! Our daughters still laugh about that one. Joe, I had never made these connections until you inquired ... interesting and thank you.

The last time I drove to the hospital, Elton John's song "Your Song" played on the radio. It made me cry a lot. When I drove to his funeral, it was playing again. This is not a song I can recall being played very regularly, and yet there it was ... twice in a space of just over one week when I was in the car.

I have heard it one other time when I was feeling particularly low and questioning my purpose in life. After informing my youngest daughter of his passing, she got in her car to meet me, and driving too fast had to brake suddenly to avoid a bird that flew toward her windscreen.

She said she felt her father go through her and knew it was him guiding the bird to slow her down.

KARREN

Author's Comments

When Karren first told me of this story, I began to think why the safari suite and the reference to the other clothes? I knew there was some type of connection there, so I got in touch with her again and inquired about those facts. Her husband in this case was showing her that not only was he still in the family's life, but he had brought his sense of humor with him. You notice the first sighting of him the day after he died. She actually laughed at his appearance as opposed to being frightened as all of us assume we would be.

The use of the song before he died was used to prep her for letting her know he was with her after he passed. The daughter realized right away that she was still being looked after, as she realized her dad had actually made her slow down while she was driving too fast after learning of his death.

Other signs

The Mammogram

I was sitting in the waiting room waiting for my semi-annual mammogram and was quite nervous this particular time. I have had an abnormal reading in the past, and I was on a twice-a-year schedule for these tests.

But all of a sudden I felt this really warm loving feeling on the left-hand side of my body. As I turned to the left, I saw an image of my deceased daughter, Suzzi, who passed over about six years ago.

She appeared glowing like an angel and had a smile I could see distinctly on her face. I felt the pressure of her hand on my shoulder and then I heard her voice in my mind say: "Mom don't worry, it will be okay". All my anxiety and stress over the situation immediately left me.

At that point, they called me and I proceeded to go into my test. As I got up to go to the other room, I noticed my daughter was no longer there, but the warm loving feeling remained. The test and follow-up tests all turned out fine, and to this day just the thought of the story brings that warm loving feeling of my deceased daughter back to me.

Susan

Author's comments

When one has contact which resonates with an actual feeling of loving energy, they can often feel it for some time afterward. Her loving daughter's support help relieve her stress.

We should all realize that, if we opened our hearts to the available loving, healing energy around us, we would have the opportunity to experience a bit of heaven.

Loving Energy

Since my husband died, I frequently feel chills, a kind of thrill really, around the back of my neck and shoulders, down my spine in various situations, and I suspect that it's him. Also, in the weeks after he died, it was almost as if he was lifting me from behind, as if his energy was supporting me.

The first time it happened was the morning after my husband died. I woke up, immediately remembered, and expected to be hit with the grief. But instead, I felt this otherworldly bliss, like a cool but not exactly physical breeze coming through me.

I have done enough meditation and energy work to know this was not from me, from my mind. It was palpable, a powerful blissful energy like nothing I've ever felt, and it lasted for a while.

Can't say exactly how long, but at least a few minutes. I had this conviction that it was him letting me know how he was feeling.

JOAN KATHERINE CRAMER

AUTHOR'S COMMENTS

Reports of this "heavenly energy" are not uncommon. Some experience this soon after a death, while others much later. I personally have experienced this, and when it happened, I remember saying that this unbelievably peaceful and loving energy will last for only a few seconds. I was surprised when it continued for about ten minutes.

Grandpa & Jake

The day my father-in-law died, we had a beautiful buck on our lawn, and I think of him every time I see one now. My lab, Jake, that passed away last year, was very close to him. He loved when grandpa would come to visit and would howl when we said grandpa is coming over.

We had an appointment to put him down, but he was so sick in the a.m. he just wanted to lay downstairs next to me. I went upstairs and thought to myself: the deer must be around waiting for him, and sure enough when I looked outside in the side yard, there were 3 deer laying down just like Jake was.

They knew it was time, and grandpa was there waiting for him.

LAURIE

AUTHOR'S COMMENTS

It is not unusual to have animals sense when others are ready to pass. The deer in this story was related to the father-in-law by the timing of his passing. So, to send a sign that he was around for this beloved pet when it was his time to pass would be a comfort to the daughter-in-law. It is fascinating how the animal world can interact with us on so many levels. Both in joy and sorrow, our pets are very intuitive and can bring great comfort to our spirit.

I'm going Too!

After our dog died, friends invited me to their house in Hawaii to stay for three weeks. My husband had been saying all year, through a Medium, that he wanted me to go to Hawaii and that he'd be going with me. First, I flew to San Diego, then to San Francisco, then Hawaii. On each flight, they announced that the plane would be full, that there would be no empty seats. There were no other empty seats on those flights, but on every single leg there was an empty seat beside me.

JOAN KATHERINE CRAMER

Author's comments

What a wonderful way to give a sign to a loved one about a trip than to have that reassurance that they too were coming along. We've all flown before! what are the chances on each leg of this happening? Especially in this day and age!

The Picture Frame

I had some framed family photos on my bedroom mantle, and my first realtor wanted me to put them away when he showed the house. So I carefully stacked them on the top shelf of a very heavy and stable bookshelf. The largest was 8.5 x11" and I had it flat on the bottom of the stack in the center of the shelf. The half dozen or so smaller photos I stacked in two piles on top of it. One day my dog and I heard a crash. We were downstairs and on the other end of the house. Couldn't figure it out. Later, we were in the bedroom and I saw that all the photos were on the floor. But the 8.5 x11 photo was still on the bottom, as if they hadn't toppled, but had instead been swept off the shelf. Only one frame had broken glass, which was amazing, as they fell on a hardwood floor. It was the only photo of my husband that was pretty unflattering. So I laughed and said: "Okay, you didn't like this one," as I threw the broken glass and the offending photo in the trash.

But behind it was a photo I didn't even remember having, and I have no idea why I might have put it behind the other one. It was the most beautiful picture of the two of us, and he has the most loving expression on his face. I had a lovely frame I wasn't using that happened to fit it perfectly — it was an odd shape — and it's the photo I now keep of us near my bedside.

JOAN KATHERINE CRAMER

Author's Comments

It is amazing how they can get our attention. Many of us have heard about things falling upright or landing a certain way, but here there was a secondary message besides the movement or sound sign. Her husband wanted to reveal the photo underneath the unflattering one of the two of them. Showing he and his love for his wife were still around.

Email from Heaven

Mentioned yesterday that my Dad has been on my mind more than usual the past couple of days. Don't know why.

Today, I got this in an email from LinkedIn. I don't use LinkedIn ... signed up a long time ago to see what it was ... but wasn't interested in it.

"Hi Carol, I'd like to connect with you on LinkedIn. Peter J. King Jr."

My Dad's name was Peter J. King Jr. ... he died two years ago! Glad you are thinking of me too Dad! XOXO

CAROL

IN MEMORY OF "MOM AND DAD"

AUTHOR'S COMMENTS

In this case, there is a combination of methods used in order for Carol to receive a sign from her deceased dad. First, her dad knew that she used email as a form of communication for her business. She always needs to stay in touch, and therefore it would be a good means to gain her attention. Her father knew there was a man, with the same name as him, sending out invitations to be in his network on the online social business company LinkedIn. So all he had to do to say "Hi" was have the man add Carol to all the invitations being sent out that day.

Then he opened his heart to his daughter, and the love flow opened her mind to thoughts of her dad. The sign was all set up, and then she got the email. Nicely done. And we all get to share in this message of love between a dad and his daughter.

The deceased do have a larger perspective of life on the Earth plane and have the ability to "multi task." They also know what multiple individuals are doing at the same time. I know this because I was shown how it works. An example is you can hear three people having conversations with three others, and you can "hear" what they're thinking at the same time even if it's not about the conversation. Also, if they're working, you can feel the connection to their actions while they talk to others. It was wild to experience that, but it was meant to teach me to understand the process.

Always Connected

Trust that your life has meaning and it will be revealed to you when the time is right.

J.M.H

Channeled by Joes Guides

We have the ability to interact with you at will. Meaning we are constantly in contact and communicating with your side. Some days are busier than others. By this we mean some days in particular, people need our connection more than others. This also is true on a larger scale, such as when there's a natural disaster or any event that includes large groups of the population.

Our communication methods between your side and outside can be quite complex at times. We realize that this communication opens up many questions from your perspective. Ethics, moral obligations, interfering in one's life and the question of free will are all brought up when people realize that we are always in communication and always in contact with your side.

But if you are allowed to glimpse the bigger picture of existence, then you'll realize that working with you is actually a continuation of the work that both sides have already agreed to do before you came to the Earth plane. The real difference between our plane and your plane is a dimensional shift in the existence and the organization of reality.

The concept and makeup of our two dimensions can be difficult to comprehend on your level. We try to teach you our methods through books such as this one. At times, we will use the scientific method to explain certain possibilities about the great whole of your environment.

But what it comes down to is we are all the same beings. Just as you have different levels of spiritual development on your plane, we also share that on our side, and that's because were all part of the same infrastructure. Earth is like a side trip the soul takes to learn and grow and experience things that they cannot understand or absorb in any other way.

If you wish to experience the duality of hate and love, suffering and compassion at its most basic level of makeup, then the Earth plane is a perfect location to experience this. There are other forms of learning that are constantly being experienced by your soul and souls on our side. These experiences are learned on a different planes of existence than the Earth plane, or even the dimension from which this information is coming. Your soul has the ability to absorb and experience new knowledge on different planes throughout time. And when we say time we mean that an all-encompassing interconnecting phase of your existence. Pieces of your soul develop on different levels throughout the time of your existence. Things you learn on the Earth plane may be used in the learning experiences as you develop into a more enlightened entity.

So we ask you to share these stories and your own personal stories with your family, friends and other loved ones in order to teach them who we all are, spiritual entities, existing together on different dimensional planes. Let your friends know that they are not alone in their experiences in anything that they take part in on the Earth plane. You are always connected to your guides, teachers and deceased loved ones.

So open your hearts, release your fear and let the contact between our side and your side flow easily, as if you're sitting with an old friend having a wonderful conversation about the existence of life.

Section V

Webpages

Make sure to sign up on the web sites to receive discounts on future products and services.

- Joehiggins.com
- Josephmhiggins.com
- Igotyourmessage.com
- Alwaysconnectedforveterans.com
- Alwaysconnectedseries.com
- Alwaysconnectedcollection.com

Web Blog: Guidance From a Higher Plane

- Joehiggins.com/blogs/blog

Other Books by Joseph M. Higgins

Hello ... Anyone Home?

A Guide on How Our Deceased Loved Ones Try to Contact Us Through the Use of Signs

By Joseph M. Higgins

Channeled insight and support from the author's guides and teachers will illuminate for you the steps by which the "other side" can communicate with every individual and how you can communicate with them!

- Have you ever dreamed of departed loved ones?
- Is it possible for the dead to communicate with us?
- Have you ever experienced smells, sounds, or electrical phenomena around you after the passing of a friend, family member, or colleague?

These might be signs that they are trying to contact you to let you know that they continue to be available to you. This book, *Hello...Anyone Home?* will teach you how to understand the process by which signs are given and received after the change known as death.

> This book lets us know that we are likely not crazy, and that these "signs" truly are our deceased loved ones speaking to us in one way or another.
>
> — L663

Available at www.amazon.com and wherever books are sold.
Available on E-readers and Audio

THE EVERYTHING GUIDE TO EVIDENCE OF THE AFTERLIFE

A SCIENTIFIC APPROACH TO PROVING THE EXISTENCE OF LIFE AFTER DEATH

BY JOSEPH M. HIGGINS & CHUCK BERGMAN

Is there life after death? Or is the end of our physical existence really the end of us? In this thought-provoking guide, you will examine scientific evidence so you can decide for yourself whether or not there is an afterlife. Medium Joseph M. Higgins and "Psychic Cop" Chuck Bergman attempt to answer questions like:

- Does consciousness survive death?
- Is communication possible between the living and dead?
- Are mediums real—or frauds?
- What happens to us during near-death experiences?
- Where do we go when we die?
- Are heaven and hell actualities?
- What is life like after death?
- Is reincarnation real—and is everyone reincarnated?

This book introduces you to the unlimited possibilities of what we face after our release from the physical world.

Available at www.amazon.com and wherever books are sold.
Available on E-readers

ALWAYS CONNECTED FOR VETERANS

DECEASED VETS GIVE GUIDANCE FROM THE OTHER SIDE

By Joseph M. Higgins
REAL ANSWERS TO TOUGH QUESTIONS

Who Are You When You Return From War?

Why Am I Alive And Not Them?

Will I Ever Find Peace?

How Will God Judge Me?

Questions veterans and their families have asked since the beginning of time, answered by vets who have been there and now have passed to the other side. With their new perspective, they reach back to help their fellow soldiers heal and gain peace with thought-provoking answers to some of the most asked questions affecting veterans.

I highly recommend this book especially to those with family in the military. It addresses so many concerns that people in the military may have about the afterlife and how their actions will affect theirs. Very well written and easy to read.

- KARL JOHNSON

Available at www.amazon.com and wherever books are sold.
Available on E-readers

www.ingramcontent.com/pod-product-compliance
Lightning Source LLC
Chambersburg PA
CBHW060518100426
42743CB00009B/1362